# The HarperCollins Concise Workbook

by

**Peter Dow Adams**
**Essex Community College**

*The HarperCollins Concise Workbook* by Peter Dow Adams.

Copyright © 1995 by HarperCollins*CollegePublishers*

ISBN: 0-06-502269-6

95 96 97 98 99 9 8 7 6 5 4 3 2 1

# TABLE OF CONTENTS

## Part VIII:   Editing:   Mechanics

# Part VII
# EDITING:
# PUNCTUATION

## Exercise 32-1:  Recognizing Sentences (32a)

Read each item below carefully.  If it is an independent clause, place brackets around it if it is not an independent clause, leave it alone.

1.   Someone rang the bell in the church.

2.   The black and white dog with the long tail.

3.   My friends are all retiring.

4.   Many of the people in the office near me.

5.   A few of the clothes in this box.

6.   My boss and her two young children.

7.   My car is broken.

8.   My suitcase is too heavy.

9.   Most of the courses at this college.

10.   The ring on the left has a sapphire stone.

# Exercise 32-2: Recognizing Fragments (32b)

Read the following paragraph carefully and underline any fragments.

Being in the army was certainly unpleasant for me. I hated everything I did for those two years. Physical training every morning at six fifteen and inspections almost every Saturday. The boredom was even worse. I spent about five hours a day just waiting. Doing nothing constructive. To make matters worse, my first sergeant hated me. When I first arrived at Fort Bragg. I dropped my rifle on his hoe. Making him my enemy for the next year. He put me on KP every weekend. Now, six years later, I still have nightmares about being in the army.

# Exercise 32-3: Finding and Revising Fragments (32b)

Correct any fragments in the following. You may be able to make corrections by crossing out or adding punctuation, or you may need to rewrite the entire sentence or cross out some words. If there is no fragment, don't change anything; just write "no fragment" at the end of the item.

1. I am developing some physical problems as I reach my forties. For example, my knees are bothering me a lot. In addition, a shortness of breath when I try to work out.

## Exercise 1-1:  Audience and Purpose (1c)

For each of the following writing situations, briefly state what the purposes of the writing might be.  Try to think of purposes other than the obvious ones. Remember that there could be more than one right answer for each of these.  The first one has been done for you.

1.  A memo to your boss suggesting several improvements in the way the office does business.

    ① to make my job easier
    ② to get a raise
    ③ to impress the boss
    ④ to make myself feel useful

2.  A cover letter to go with your resume to a personnel office of a company where you could like to work.




3.  A note to the owner of a parked car that you have just backed into, denting the fender.

1

4. A letter to your parents telling them you have a summer job in New York City that starts June 3 and that as a result you will be seeing them from May 25 to June 1.

5. A paper for your psychology teacher in which you propose to revise Freud's theories by adding the concept of a "super-id" to parallel the superego. (Never mind that you may not know what a superego is, and that the "super-id" is a term we made up for this example. What would be the purpose of such a piece of writing?)

# Exercise 2-1: Focusing: Subject and Thesis (2b)

Use what you have learned about theses to evaluate each of the following. If it is a good thesis, leave it alone. If it is weak, revise it to make an effective thesis.

1. Religion in America will be the focus of this paper.

2. Lyndon Johnson was the president who first committed American troops in Vietnam.

3. Required courses are opposed by many.

4. Who really assassinated President Kennedy?

5. Violence on TV provides a harmless outlet for the natural violence we all sometimes feel.

6. Something must be done about the divorce rate in this country.

7. People disagree about the wisdom of leaving children in day-care centers.

8. The causes of the Civil War.

9. The dangers of genetic engineering.

10. The average doctor's salary is greater than $120,000 per year.

# Exercise 2-2:  Focusing Subject and Thesis (2b)

In the last exercise, you revised our theses.  In this exercise, you will write some of your own.  Write a thesis statement for each of the following topics.

1. teachers' salaries

2. smoking in public places

3. replacement of human workers by robots

4. 55 mph speed limit

5. ambition

# Exercise 3-1:
# Distinguishing between Generalizations and Evidence (3b)

Read the following paragraphs and underline any assertions. For each paragraph, in the space provided, list briefly the points that support the assertion. (If there is no evidence to support the assertion, leave the space blank.) Check the appropriate space to indicate whether the assertion is adequately supported or not. The first one is done for you.

1. <u>Chincoteague Island is a great place for a family vacation.</u> The beach there is one of the prettiest on the East Coast, and it's not too crowded. Besides the beach, there are miles of bike trails that are beautiful and, most important, level. The birds at Chincoteague are among the most impressive anywhere. In one afternoon, I saw a great blue heron, a little green heron, a glossy ibis, and three kinds of egrets. Finally, the motel where we stay has a swimming pool, a tennis court, and a weight-lifting room.

a. *pretty beach*

b. *not crowded beach*

c. *bike trails*

d. *bird-watching*

e. *motel with pool, tennis, weight lifting*

f. _____

g. _____

h. _____

✓ adequate support    ___ inadequate support

2. First, I overslept this morning and therefore, didn't have time to take a shower. Then, the toast got stuck in the toaster and burned up. To make matters worse, it was the last piece of bread in the house. So, I decided to drink my coffee as I drove to work. But when I tried to start my car, the battery was dead. After a half-hour, my neighbor managed to get it started with a jump from his battery. I arrived at work an hour late and quite frazzled. it was a terrible morning.

a. _____

b. _____

c. _____

d. _____

e. _____

f. _____

g. _____

h. _____

____ adequate support      ____ inadequate support


3. Something has to be done about terrorism. Madmen cannot be allowed to get away with things they have been doing. Terrorists must learn that there is a price to be paid for violating the laws of natural decency. It's time we stopped letting these thugs push us around. It's time America took a stand.

a. _____

b. _____

c. _____

d. _____

e. _____

**f.** _____

**g.** _____

**h.** _____

___ adequate support     ___ inadequate support

4. The local news on Channel 4 is a joke. Even the newscasters don't seem to take it seriously. They hardly ever cover any real news; the show is almost all sensationalism. and the reporters are incompetent. They don't even understand the stories they are covering. The always ask the people they are interviewing dumb questions. The show is so bad that I watch it only for laughs.

**a.** _____

**b.** _____

**c.** _____

**d.** _____

**e.** _____

**f.** _____

**g.** _____

**h.** _____

___ adequate support     ___ inadequate support

5. American society is getting older. The percentage of Americans over seventy has doubled since 1960. There are twice as many people between

the ages of fifty and seventy as there were in 1960. And, even the number between thirty and fifty is increasing, up 20 percent in the same time period. The only age groups that have a smaller percentage now than in 1960 are those below thirty. The twenty to thirty age group is down 16 percent, and the under twenty group down 28 percent.

a. _____

b. _____

c. _____

d. _____

e. _____

f. _____

g. _____

h. _____

____ adequate support     ____ inadequate support

6. This town is in better shape than it's been in for the last twenty five years. mayor Washington reports that the average income is at its highest level ever. He further points out that unemployment is at 6 1/2 percent, the lowest since 1967. Chief of Police Daniels has repeatedly observed that the crime rate is lower than at any time since 1962. The president of the Chamber of Commerce has announced that this year will be the best business year the town has experienced in twenty years; sixteen new businesses have opened, and only two have gone out of business in the past twelve months. Even the president of the PTA has good news. Or children's scores on the College Boards have gone up for the past three years in a row, after fifteen years of decline. Everywhere you look, this town is really improving.

a. _____

**b.** _____

**c.** _____

**d.** _____

**e.** _____

**f.** _____

**g.** _____

**h.** _____

___ adequate support     ___ inadequate support

7. Living in the city has many advantages for me. All my ordinary needs can be satisfied within two blocks of my apartment building. There is a supermarket across the street and a dry cleaners just down the block. A large movie house with four different theaters is located two blocks away, and my doctor's office is right in my building. Getting around in the city is easy and inexpensive. One block from my house, I can catch a bus that takes me right to Memorial Hospital, where I work. By walking another block, I can catch another bus that takes me all the way downtown for shopping, dinner, of the theater. City transportation is so convenient that I don't even need a car. But most important, I love meeting lots of interesting people. The other night I couldn't sleep, so I went across the street to a cafe and found myself in a great conversation for two hours.

**a.** _____

**b.** _____

**c.** _____

**d.** _____

**e.** _____

**f.** _____

**g.** _____

**h.** _____

___ adequate support    ___ inadequate support

# Part II
# DRAFTING AND REVISING: PARAGRAPHS THAT WORK

## Exercise 7-1:
## The Paragraph as a Unit of Thought (7a and b)

Read the following paragraphs and cross out any sentences that do not support the topic sentence. If possible, work on the exercise in peer groups.

### Paragraph 1

Making vegetarian tacos is easy if you follow my recipe. First, you empty a pint of cottage cheese into a mixing bowl. Next, pour in two tablespoons of anise seeds; then, add a cup of raisins. Finally, chop up about two cups of green onions and add half to the cottage cheese mixture. I first ate green onions when I was in the army. Stir the mixture and use it to stuff six taco shells. Place the shells in a large baking dish and cover with grated Swiss cheese, taco sauce, and the remaining green onions. Bake the tacos at 350 degrees for about fifteen minutes.

### Paragraph 2

I worry about what any present I buy will mean to the person I give it to. For example, my sister has always had an inferiority complex because she didn't go to college. If I buy her anything for the kitchen, will she get the idea that I think of her main interest as cooking? Instead, if I buy her a book of T.S. Eliot's poetry, will she think I am trying to educate her? Eliot wrote poetry in which he described modern society as a wasteland.

And my mother is just as bad as my sister, only her touchy point is her age. If I buy her a tennis racket, Ill worry that it's too young for her. If I get her a pair of Isotoner gloves, I'll be concerned that only "senior citizens" wear Isotoners. Because I worry so much over every gift, it usually takes me a full weekend to buy anything.

**Paragraph 3**

You are probably aware that, for most trips, it is cheaper to go by train than it is to fly. Did you also know that it can be faster? If you count the time spent getting to the airport and waiting for the plane, trips under five hundred miles can be quicker by train. In addition, train travel is the safest means of transportation. Even when train accidents do occur, seldom are passengers injured. Many people also find traveling by train to be psychologically more satisfying. Of course, psychologists sometimes have fairly "far out" ideas about things; everyone has heard of Freud's theories about boys wanting to kill their fathers and make love with their mothers. But on this matter of flying, I think they're right. If you've watched miles of countryside go by your window, you really feel more satisfaction with the trip; somehow, flying above the clouds makes it hard to believe you've really traveled. Further, most people find riding a train more pleasant. Every time I've taken the train, I've met people whom I enjoyed talking with. That never happens to me on a plane. And finally, have you ever heard of a train being hijacked? So all things considered, there are many advantages to traveling by train.

# Exercise 8-1: Providing Transitions (8a)

Read the following paragraphs and decide which one is more effective. In the space below, tell how the paragraphs differ and why one is more effective. If possible, discuss this exercise in peer groups.

**Paragraph 1**

I have several good reasons for not going to work today. I was stung several times in the foot by bees while walking in my yard last night. I cannot get my shoe on. My son is staying home from school. He has a bad cold. The computer is being repaired at work. I wouldn't be able to get much done anyhow.

**Paragraph 2**

I have several good reasons for not going to work today. First, I was stung several times in the foot by bees while walking in my yard last night. As a result, I cannot get my shoe on. Next, my son is staying home from school because he has a bad cold. Finally the computer is being repaired at work, so I wouldn't be able to get much done anyhow.

_____

_____

_____

_____

# Exercise 8-2: Providing Transitions (8a)

You are undoubtedly already familiar with many transitional works and phrases. This exercise will give you some sense of how many you know. following each sentence, write as many transitional expressions as you can think of that would work gracefully in the blank space. (We have provided a blank for every

transitional expression we could think of.  don't feel you have to think of exactly
that many;  just fill in as many as you can.)

1.  I am not going out tonight.    My car is not running well;
    _____, the forecast is for snow.

    _____          _____

    _____          _____

    _____          _____


2.  She wore a clove of garlic around her neck; _____, she was
    never attacked by a vampire.

    _____          _____

    _____          _____

    _____          _____


3.  I studied hard for my astrology test; _____, I failed it.

    _____          _____


4.  I am allergic to many things; _____, I break out in a rash
    whenever I am around aardvarks.

    _____          _____

    _____          _____


14

5. Emily made lemonade; _____, she took the cat for a swim.

_____        _____

_____        _____

_____        _____

# Exercise 9-1:  Avoiding Shifts in Tense (9a)

Proofread the following paragraph carefully and correct any errors.  All errors involve inconsistent verb tense.

Looking for a prom dress with my daughter was quite an experience. She announced that the girls in her school had decided they would not wear "real" prom dresses.  Then she tries to explain what they would wear, but I couldn't understand it.  We went to a huge mall with four major department stores.  After five hours, I had held up forty-one dresses and asked, "Would you like something like this?"  And the answer is consistently "No." So we try a fancy ladies' dress shop, but nothing there will do.  After a break for dinner, we drive to last department store in town, but nothing there will do either.  Finally, we stopped at one last dress shop, and there she finds the dress she wanted.  It was a white strapless dress with a lot of gauzy material around the bottom.  I could not see how it was any different from a traditional prom dress, but I am so relieved to have found a dress that I do not say a word.

# Exercise 9-2:
# Avoiding Shifts in Person and Number (9b)

Revise the following paragraphs for shifts in person and number.

### Paragraph 1

Most people find the novels of James Michener easy to read and interesting. They enjoy his tales because they are set in exotic places like Hawaii, Spain, and Africa. Readers find his characters convincing and complex and his stories exciting and hard to predict. Once you start a Michener novel, you will have trouble putting it down. This can be risky because they are usually more than six hundred pages long.

### Paragraph 2

You will find using a word processor to be much easier than you think. You merely type your paper using the keyboard of the computer exactly like a typewriter. Then, the writer uses a various combinations of keys to make changes in his or her paper. He or she can move words around, erase words, and insert words with just the flick of a key. The writer who has used a word processor will never go back to an old-fashioned typewriter.

**Paragraph 3**

People who win large prizes in lotteries often find that all that money only makes them miserable. They have to put up with a lot of people trying to get their hands on a chunk of the money. They may even find that their friends expect them to share the prize money. All these pressures take a lot of the fun out of winning. You discover that you can no longer trust anyone. You have to be on your guard constantly to make sure you aren't taken advantage of. You no longer can relax and enjoy life.

# Exercise 9-3:
# Avoiding Shifts in Mood and Voice (9c and 9d)

Correct the mood and voice errors in the following paragraph.

Most people agree on the basics of car maintenance. For example, change your oil every 3,000 miles, and at the same time you should check your tire pressure and tread wear. Other fluids, such as anti-freeze, brake and transmission fluids, should be added if necessary. But don't stop there. Mechanics recommend that filters and belts are checked regularly. One garage owner said that if he was me, he wouldn't drive a car with dirty filters or squealing belts. Careful car owners also know to keep a maintenance record. A complete upkeep and repair log is jotted down there, a practice which helps them operate their vehicles more efficiently. Maintaining a car isn't difficult, as long as it is done conscientiously and consistently. It will extend your car's life, and your headaches may be decreased as well.

# Part III
# DRAFTING AND REVISING: EFFECTIVE SENTENCES

## Exercise 11-1: Coordinating Equal Ideas (11a)

Choose the correct conjunction from the pairs in parenthesis.

1. This morning's hard rain suddenly stopped, (and, but) the skies cleared, (and, so) I decided to take the afternoon off.

2. The air is wonderfully fresh, (but, so) I can't decide whether I should ride my bike or go for a hike.

3. Each is appealing in its own way, (for, yet) I think I'll ride my bike.

4. Afterward, I'll probably read for while, (or, nor) I'll listen to music.

5. And around dinner time, I'll have to decide what I want to eat, (but, yet) I'll worry about that later.

# Exercise 11-2:
# Subordinating Less Important Ideas (11b)

Rewrite these sentences so the less important ideas are subordinate.

1. My English teacher just won the National Book Award and returned our research papers.

2. Tawanda bought a new puppy and is wearing a red sweater.

3. The fire began in the basement and is of suspicious origins.

4. Investigators from the fire department discovered oil-soaked rags in the basement, and they spent six hours probing the wreckage.

5. The family had lived in the house for fifteen years and were planning to move in about three weeks.

# Exercise 12-1:
# Correcting Faulty Parallelism (12a-f)

Proofread the following sentences and correct any errors. All errors involve faulty parallelism.

1. Helen's children expect her to drive them to school, take them to after-school activities, and to have dinner ready when it's convenient for them.

2. This weekend we did some reading, went to a movie, and Tommy's party.

3. When Terry broke up with Michael, he sulked for weeks, he talked about her all the time, and didn't go out with anyone else for six months.

4. Julian's plan was to finish his research, write his note cards, and to complete a rough draft of his term paper by the first of March.

5. When he arrived at my house, Craig's clothes were covered with mud, he had a cut over his eye, and he was grinning like a fool.

6. Students in this class are gaining confidence and enthusiasm for writing.

7. Dishonesty has and will continue to be destructive to relationships.

8. Having studied the piano for five years and she had sung in her church choir since she was eight, so she had no trouble getting an A in Music 101.

9. Josh moved to our town, he dated six different women in the first six months, and then disappeared without a trace.

10. So far in this class, we studied the Greeks, Romans, and the Middle Ages.

# Exercise 13-1:
# Avoiding Misplaced Modifiers (13a-e)

Proofread the following sentences and correct any errors. All errors involve misplaced modifiers.

1. Having my tax return prepared by an accountant, the bill was eighty-five dollars.

2. Walking past the lake, spring finally made its appearance.

3. Hoping the rain would stop, we went ahead with the panic.

4. Arriving early at my office, the door was locked.

5. Whistling quietly, she was getting on everyone's nerves.

6. To read in a car, the road must be smooth.

7. Driving a motorcycle for the first time, my dog ran right in front of me.

8. Running in the marathon, Melia sprained her ankle.

9. Cowering under my car, I spotted the missing cat.

10. Searching through his pockets, Timothy begged the bus driver to wait a minute.

# Exercise 15-1:
# Avoiding Mixed and Incomplete Constructions (15 a-e)

Proofread the following sentences and correct any errors. All errors involve mixed or incomplete constructions.

1.  Although I had a seen the movie, but I told Oleana I would go with her.

2.  The reason for the mistake was because Lonny didn't understand what you wanted him to do.

3.  An opera is when you have singing or classical music and at least some acting out of the scenes.

4.  The purpose of this book is designed to explain the rules of grammar.

5.  The teacher in my math class she gives far too much homework.

6.  I took a course in which was more difficult than I realized.

7.  Alvin's wife was angry and disappointed in him.

8.  Carl is more successful than anyone from his high school.

9. Luis has discovered writing is important to success in the business world.

10. By sending the application meant that I would soon be enrolled in a rehabilitation program.

# Part IV
# DRAFTING AND REVISING: EFFECTIVE WORD CHOICE

## Exercise 16-1:  Choosing Effective Words (16a)

The following sentences contain errors involving the use of homonyms. Proofread them and correct any errors.  Each sentence may contain no errors, one error, or more than one error.

1.  I hope this letter doesn't arrive to late too help you with your project.

2.  Even though the driver applied her breaks gradually, the truck spun out of control.

3.  If I haven't past this course, I don't no what I will tell my parents.

4.  If you here anything knew about the election, give me a call.

5.  There are to many patience in this hospital right now.

6.  Julie's personnel goals do not include having children.

7.  Shirley used to no more than I did about literature, and she was a better writer to.

8.  When I past that truck, the driver flashed his lights at me.

9.  If you set that pot down hear, I will take care of the rest of the meal.

10. This job requires to much patients for me.


# Exercise 16-2:  Choosing Effective Words (16a)

Proofread the following sentences and correct any errors.  The errors will involve mistakes in usage.

1.  It will be find with me if your brother comes to.

2.  The effect of her decision is that were going to get a new computer.

3.  I don't no weather Karl understands what a mess his llama makes with its continual spitting.

4.  Donna is know better at swimming then John is.

5.  I'll bet Yolanda will loose that application before she fills it out.

6.  Michael made up his mine and past the reading coarse in one semester.

7.  Do you know if this hotel has a nice restaurant were we can have a little quite talk?

8.  Accept for Monday, the weather was really find while we were at the Cape.

9. I wish I new how to brake this news to my parents.

10. I would rather lose the contest then be thought of as a cheater.

11. Mark came hear, ate his dinner, and than left without eating desert.

12. Your advice had a good effect on Joan's attitude.

13. If I haven't passed statistics this time, I'll lose my mine.

14. When the weather is hot, you should we're lose clothes.

15. Were not sure if staying home wouldn't be a better idea then going to the picnic.

16. She went to the personal office to find out about her retirement benefits.

17. There are too reasons why this restaurant is better then Vallegio's.

18. I didn't here from the teacher, so I guess I past the course.

19. The affect of his insecurity is that he has very little patience.

20. I can't quiet except his explanation for his mistake; it's not like him.

# Exercise 16-3:  Choosing Effective Words (16a)

Proofread the following sentences and correct any errors.  The errors will involve mistakes in usage.

1.  This medicine is not suppose to make you sleepy.

2.  I fine that I like most foods once I get use to them.

3.  The weather could of been alot better, but we had a good time anyhow.

4.  Were worried about the affect this experience may have on her career.

5.  The knew cafeteria is alright, but it could of been alot better.

6.  We should of gone too a Chinese restaurant because Mary likes Chinese food much better then Italian.

7.  To help you quite smoking, perhaps you should try and eat an apple whenever you feel like a cigarette.

8.  Students are suppose too read a chapter of the text each week.

9.  We would of been hear an hour ago, but we had a flat tire.

10.  I think Joe could of past this coarse, accept for the statistics.

11.  Is it alright with you if I take tomorrow off to take care of a personnel problem I am having with my ex-husband.

12. Troy use to live in Phoenix until he quite his job and moved back here.

13. Penny said she should try and remember too bring your binoculars tomorrow.

14. Two dollars would of been enough for a tip; the desert was terrible.

15. It is really to hot for Camilla to walk over here.

16. We didn't want to loose the game, but they we're just to good for us.

17. The whether this summer is going to brake the record for heat.

18. Do you mine if Robin and Norm try and fine her earring.

19. There are alot of mistakes in my essay, but Mr. Cimino passed it anyway.

20. It is alright if they make fun of me; I'm use to it.

# Exercise 16-4:  Choosing Effective Words (16a)

Proofread the following essay and correct any errors. All errors involve confusing words.

My brother went too West Point, and he hated every minute of it.  He should of known that he wouldn't like all that discipline, but he didn't really think alot about it before he went.  When he was a junior, he wrote a essay on Herman

Melville's *Moby Dick*.  He was depressed when he got it back with an F on it. Even though he past the course, I don't think he ever forgave that professor or West Point for that grade.

A few months later, he resigned an transferred too Virginia Tech.  After a year there, he disappeared and, six months later, reappeared living in New York, married, and enrolled in Columbia.  At Columbia he majored in English and got straight A's.  I don't no weather it was New York, marriage, or Columbia, but something sure had a good affect on him.

In his last semester before graduation, he took a seminar on Melville.  For that course, he had too do a paper on one of Melville's novels, so he pulled out his old paper from West Point.  Now he did retype the paper and correct a few obvious typos, but he submitted basically the same paper he had turned in several years earlier at West Point.  Of course, he new he wasn't suppose to do this, but he just wanted to prove how wrong those military instructors had been.  After waiting about to weeks, he got the paper back, and he got an "F" on it at Columbia also.

Now he thinks there was some kind of conspiracy.

# Part V
# GRAMMAR: UNDERSTANDING BASIC CONCEPTS

## Exercise 19-1: Recognizing Nouns (19a)

In the following sentences, underline all nouns. Each sentence may contain no nouns, one noun, or more than one noun.

1. Marc's problem is he never reads his homework assignments.

2. Two cardinals flew into the window of my living room.

3. My quarrel with the boss was about the length of my vacation.

4. A lunch of salad and soup does not have many calories.

5. Chris's stereo does not play tapes.

6. We walked around until we became nervous because it was too late.

7. My dog sleeps at the foot of my bed.

8. Communication is important to a good relationship.

9. A school bus had broken down in the left lane.

10. Her desk is located in the corner of her bedroom.

# Exercise 19-2: Recognizing Pronouns (19b)

In the following sentences, underline all pronouns. Each sentence may contain no pronouns, one pronoun, or more than one pronoun.

1. We should buy some of their strawberries because they are on sale.

2. Carl was helping himself to the desserts.

3. Everybody brought something to the party.

4. Ruth gave us good advice.

5. These are Debbie's shoes.

6. Tim and Gail said they would be here by nine o'clock.

7.  The movie that we saw was about the town that we had grown up in.


8.  Most of the children don't believe in Santa Claus, but many of them
    pretend that they do.


9.  Linda gave herself a hard time because she didn't get the hob.


10. Half of the children had colds, but that didn't slow them down.


# Exercise 19-3:   Recognizing Verbs (19c)

In the following paragraph, underline all verbs twice.

Nathaniel Hawthorne's novel *The Scarlet Letter* tells the story of Hester
Prynne.  Hester was a young woman living in Boston in the colonial days of the
Massachusetts Bay Colony.  She was married to a much older scholar.  Her
husband had not yet come over from England.  Despite her marriage, she fell in
love with Arthur Dimmesdale, a popular minister in the Puritan church.  She and
Arthur made love once.  Unfortunately, she became pregnant.  In puritanical
Boston, such behavior was both sinful and illegal.  The church elders demanded the
name of the father of Hester's child, but Hester would not identify him, and
Dimmesdale did not identify himself.  As a result, Hester spent a term in prison and
was then required to wear a scarlet letter A on the breast of her dress for the rest of

her life.  On the day of her entry into prison, her husband arrived in Boston in

disguise.  He quickly understood the situation and fairly soon identified the father.

He then tormented the remorseful  and sickly Dimmesdale to the point of death.

Finally, Dimmesdale confessed his sin at a public gathering and died on the spot.

Hester remained in Boston and converted her scarlet letter into a symbol of honor

and goodness, through her kindness to others, especially troubled women.

# Exercise 19-4:
# Distinguishing Verbs and Verbals (19c)

Underline the verbs twice and subjects once in the following sentences.  Be careful
not confuse verbs and verbals.

1.   To get into the dance required a ticket.

2.   Finding a key in my purse is not easy.

3.   Hoping for a miracle, I turned in my test.

4.   To get a job, Paul mailed over one hundred resumes.

5.   Greg was working on a degree in engineering.

6.   Looking to his left, Kent did not notice the approaching truck.

7.   To get to Kay's house is easy.

8.   To mail that letter will require four stamps.

9.   Cleaning the bathroom, Tom found his wallet.

10.   To raise tomatoes, one must have lots of sun.

11.   Running several miles a day is good for your heart.

12.   Sitting at my typewriter, I found peace of mind.

13.   Steven wanted to finish his paper by Friday's class.

14.   To reach the ocean by noon was our plan.

15.   Forcing the lock, Robin broke her key.

16.   Holding my head made my headache a lot better.

17.   To fix my zipper, I needed three hands.

18.   To teach her cat a lesson, Helene tied his paws together.

19.   Telling Jackie about the death of her mother was not easy.

20.   To cover his mistake, Jeff had to tell several lies.

# Exercise 19-5: Recognizing Parts of Speech (19d-g)

In the following sentences, underline the adjectives and write *adj* above them; underline the adverbs and write *adv* above them.

1.   Last evening I saw a really beautiful sunset.

2.   The colors, multi-hued and impressive, quickly filled the western sky.

3.   Undoubtedly, it was the best sunset I have ever seen.

4.   Amazingly, it completely transformed the somewhat dejected mood I had been

     experiencing.

5.   It was over in about ten minutes, leaving me to silently wonder if anyone else had

     witnessed it.

In the following sentences, underline the prepositions.

6.   Turn left at the second traffic light.

7.   My apartment building is up the hill on the right.

8.   It's the one across the street from the pink house with blue shutters.

9. My apartment is the one below the balcony with hundreds of plants on it.

10. Since it is easy to find, you won't have any trouble.

In the following sentences, underline the coordinating conjunctions and write *coord* over them; underline the subordinating conjunctions and write *sub* over them.

11. Friday or Saturday will be fine for our party.

12. Before we can invite anyone else, we will need to check with Harriet to see if she can come.

13. We have to make sure she can come, since the party is in her honor.

14. I will make a cake, so why don't you bring the ice cream.

15. If she can't come Friday or Saturday, we will have to delay the party until the following week.

# Exercise 20-1:
# Recognizing Subjects and Verbs (20 a-b)

In the following sentences, underline all verbs twice and all subjects once.

1. My typewriter has been cleaned.

2. Joanne and her husband took a trip to Wyoming and saw grizzly bears.

3. Were some of your answers wrong?

4. There were two reasons for her anger.

5. Send your order to the following address.

6. A friend of my sister is the president of CBS.

7. One of the boys was selected for the show.

8. Jim and Cathy will not be coming to the meeting.

9. In my bed was a gray, striped, furry animal.

10. Helen and a neighbor of hers will be waiting for us at the station.

11. Has Monique booked a reservation for the whole group?

12. The man in the checked suit and the striped tie is my uncle.

13. One section of the roof of my new house is tile.

14. My little sister and her friend stayed up late and watched television.

15. In a few minutes, we should leave for the movie.

16. The cover of my typewriter was lying on the floor.

17. Get a firm grip on yourself.

18. Is the handle of the lawn mower broken?

19. There are always exceptions to grammar rules.

20. One of the boys and none of the girls remembered the name of the teacher.

# Exercise 20-2:
# Recognizing Parts of Sentences (20 c, d, e, i, and j)

Underline the direct and indirect objects in the following sentences.

1. Bart gave his neighbor a valentine.

2. Jeff's dog ate a bone.

3. Sue sent me an e-mail message about her new job.

4. The company received a phone call from an irate customer.

5. Larry showed Marcia how determined he was.

Underline the prepositional phrases in the following sentences.

6. In the library are many books about Thomas Jefferson.

7. The car is parked near the back door.

8. Without a doubt, the keys were in the drawer where I put them.

9. Their destination was around the bend in the road.

10. The cat on that hot tin roof is mine.

Underline the independent clauses below. Each item may have no independent clauses, one independent clause, or more than one.

11. My feet smell.

12. Craig opened the door, and Nessie walked into the room wearing a large hat.

13. The president and most of the members of his cabinet.

14. Maxine sat down at her computer and typed in the first line of her paper.

15. When I arrived at the small store with a striped awning in front.

Underline the dependent clauses in the following. Each item may have no dependent clauses, one dependent clause, or more than one.

16. If you know the way, I will ride with you.

17. The woman who lives next to me is moving to California when she sells her house.

18. Because Julio took five courses and because he is very good at math, he is getting straight A's this semester.

19. Thinking he had made a mistake, George left the meeting without saying a word.

20. I gave my paper to the man who is standing next to the window.

# Part VI
# EDITING:
# GRAMMAR

## Exercise 21-1: Basic Subject-Verb Agreement (21a)

Correct any errors in the following. All errors involve subject-verb agreement. Each sentence may contain no errors, one error, or more than one error.

1. My brother often drives to school.

2. Teachers sometimes gives a lot of homework on weekends.

3. Tony lend me his bicycle every Friday.

4. My dog wakes me up every morning.

5. This computer check the spelling of my papers.

6. The supermarket charges more for the basics each week.

7. That song remind me of my first wife.

8. Often, the Murphy kids visits their grandparents.

9. Three students comes in late each class.

10.    These envelopes contain bonus checks for every employee.

11.    This toaster work well on English muffins.

12.    The furnace at our apartment burns a lot of oil.

13.    My favorite show come on at ten o'clock on Tuesday nights.

14.    The baby seldom sleep past seven in the morning.

15.    My aunts always hugs everyone.

16.    That teacher gives low grades to most students.

17.    My alarm ring at seven every morning.

18.    The bank open at 9:30 on Saturdays.

19.    Her parties always ends by midnight.

20.    This stapler sometimes chews up the paper.

# Exercise 21-2:
# Subject-Verb Agreement with the Verb *to be* (21d)

The following sentences are all written in the past tense. Rewrite them in the present tense.

1.    My answer was just a guess.

2.     The suspect's car was a late model Buick.

3.     They were my best cuff links.

4.     Marcy was living with her parents.

5.     Terry was my best friend, but I was angry at her.

6.     You were not welcome here.

7.     Ned risked his life when he jumped from the plane.

8.     I was surprised by the ending of the novel.

9.     We were pleased with the work.

10.    The students were angry with the dean.

# Exercise 21-3:
# Subject-Verb Agreement with Helping Verbs (21e)

The following sentences have plural subjects. Rewrite each of them in the space provided with the singular subject indicated. Be sure to check for subject-verb agreement. The first one done for you.

1.	Jim and Jean can give me a ride to school tomorrow.

	Jim *can give me a ride to school tomorrow.*

2.	My parents must worry a lot about my little sister.

	My mother _____

3.	The teachers are hoping that the school has a snow day soon.

	The teacher _____

4.	Those dogs may be lost.

	That dog _____

5.	My friends will lend me the money.

	My friend _____

6.	Mr. and Ms. Caprio have opened a store.

	Ms. Caprio _____

7.	Gayle and her sister should be here soon.

	Gayle _____

8. Ford and Chrysler are bringing out new models in January.

    Ford _____

9. The mayor and his staff can influence the vote.

    The mayor _____

10. My enemies would love to find out my plan.

    My enemy _____

# Exercise 21-4:
# Subject-Verb Agreement with Past and Future Tenses (21f)

The following paragraph is written in the past tense. In the space provided, rewrite it in the future tense. The first sentence has been done for you.

Even though I retired last May, the summer was busy. My car was paid for, and my mortgage was paid off, so my expenses were minimal. I was working part time for a landscaping company, which meant lots of sun, fresh air, and exercise. With my spare time, I took a computer programming course at the local college. It was wonderful to take a course just out of intellectual curiosity. I also planted a good sized vegetable garden in my backyard. Besides all that, I saw every movie that came to town.

*Even though I will retire next May, the summer will be busy.*

_____

_____

_____

_____

_____

_____

_____

_____

_____

_____

_____

## Exercise 21-5:
## Subject-Verb Agreement with Phrases that Come between Subject and Verb (21g), with Compound Subjects (21h), and with the Subject Following the Verb (21k)

Correct any subject-verb agreement errors in the following sentences. Each sentence may have no errors, one error, or more than one error.

1. The lights on the ocean liner is visible for miles

2. The papers in this box belongs to my grandmother.

3. A friend of my parents sends them oranges from Florida every winter.

4. The color of her eyes are a deep blue.

5.   A list of these times is located on the desk at the front of the room.

6.   There is three choices for dessert.

7.   In the closet are my winter clothes.

8.   Val's problem with languages is that she cannot remember vocabulary.

9.   There are a good reason for Jay's decision.

10.  In the box is my good shoes.

11.  John and his dog is running in the park.

12.  A mouse or a rat is chewing the boxes in the basement.

13.  Val or her brothers gives me a tennis lesson every weekend.

14.  The teacher or the students is going to apologize.

15.  The players and the coach are angry at the newspaper.

# Exercise 21-6:
# Subject-Verb Agreement with Indefinite Pronouns (21i), with Collective Nouns (21j), and with Linking Verbs (21l)

Correct any errors in the following sentences. All errors will involve subject-verb agreement. Each sentence may contain no errors, one error, or more than one error.

1.  Each of those paintings are on sale for under two hundred dollars.

2.  The crowd were impatient for the game to start.

3.  The winners of the talent contest was a pair of singers from California.

4.  Everyone of the students were studying for the exam.

5.  A number of books was piled up on the teacher's desk.

6.  A pair of kittens has taken over my life.

7.  Someone were standing in the street yelling last night at 2:00.

8.  Either of the answers are correct.

9.  A flock of egrets land at the creek near my house every morning.

10.  Each of the books on the syllabus are more than three hundred pages long.

11.  Hank's favorite dessert now that he is off his diet are strawberries and cream.

12.  Everyone in my 8:00 class have been late at least once this semester.

13.  The number of problems on the homework was astounding.

14.  Everybody that I know have already seen that movie.

15. Much of the trouble was caused by our inability to speak Spanish.

16. A source of pollution that many people are not aware of are the many farms in the state.

17. Most of the cookies was gone by the time Leon walked into the kitchen.

18. My normal lunch these days are a couple of crackers.

19. Either of the cars were too expensive for Sam's budget.

20. The title of the book Mark chose to read were *Ten Ways to Lower Your Income Taxes*.

# Exercise 21-7:
# Subject-Verb Agreement in Clauses Beginning with *Who*, *Which*, or *That* (21m) and When the Subject is Plural in Form but Singular in Meaning (21n)

Correct any errors in the following sentences. All errors will involve subject-verb agreement. Each sentence may contain no errors, one error, or more than one error.

1. Teachers who has too many students cannot do a good job.

2. General Motors are laying off another six thousand employees.

3. Netitia is the only one of those women who are learning to ride a bike.

4.  Physics are extremely hard if you don't understand calculus.

5.  *For Whom the Bell Tolls* is one of those books that reminds me of my father.

6.  Ten dollars were more than I expected for a tip from that table full of drunks.

7.  Gregor is one of those men who always reminds me of an insect.

8.  The news from my wife's business is not very encouraging.

9.  Kathy bought a car that have ninety thousand miles on it.

10. Four miles are long enough to walk on your first day back.

# Exercise 21-8:
# Review of Subject-Verb Agreement (21a-n)

Correct any errors in the following essay. All errors will involve subject-verb agreement.

Human beings has very complicated attitudes toward work. To start with, each of us are not even sure what we mean by the word. Sometimes we use it to mean anything that require an exertion of physical energy like moving heavy equipment or loading a moving van. But playing tennis requires exertion, and most of us does not consider tennis work. And what about office work? That doesn't require much physical energy, but most of us consider it work. What about mowing the lawn or shoveling snow? Since we usually aren't paid for these, most of us don't think of such household chores as work. On the other hand, if someone get paid for winning the lottery, we wouldn't consider that work. To keep things simple, for the next few minutes, I will use *work* to refer to any activity for which someone earn money; for the purposes of this discussion, I won't consider money won in contests as *earned*.

Work is something most of us would like to avoid. As far back as Adam and Eve, work was seen as a curse, a punishment. Everyone I know love a day off from work. When a huge snowstorm or a power failure cause work to be canceled, everyone celebrates. Further, vacation time is an important part of the compensation we get for our jobs. Many of us spends our hard earned cash to buy "labor saving" devices, which is supposed to reduce the amount of work we do. It do seem that we wants to avoid work.

At the same time, however, work is an important part of our lives. For many people, it is the way they define who they are. Ask an American what someone "is," and the answer is usually something like, "She is a lawyer," or "He is a teacher" rather than "She is a Buddhist," or "He is a socialist." The importance of work in our lives becomes even clearer when someone lose his or her job. Of course, when people are laid off, they lose their salaries, but being laid off also means, for many people, losing a sense of who they are. For many people, being unemployed is rough on their self-esteem.

There is many reasons why work is so important in our lives. For one thing, work often is what gives meaning to our lives. Work, when we are lucky, allows us to feel we are making some contribution to society. Through work, many of us gain a sense of success. Doing a job well makes us feel we are contributing to society.

Also, work provides a social outlet. Despite warnings that it is unwise to date anyone at work, the workplace is where many single people meet and form relationships. And for many of us, work has become the primary site of our social interaction. There is great satisfactions to be experienced from day-to-day contact with our fellow workers. We form friendships at work. We has fights and we makes up. In many cases, the workplace has replaced the extended family as the primary location of social interaction.

Finally, we go to work because we would feel strange if we didn't. Going to work is what adults do in our society. In the past, this was true primarily for men, but today it has become true for most women as well. If we stay home from work on a weekday, anyone who see us will assume we are sick. Going to work is normal.

No matter how good a day off feels, no matter how much we complain about our jobs, work seems to have become something we can't live without.

# Exercise 22-1:
# Making Sure that a Pronoun Has One Clear Antecedent (22a) and Making Sure that a Pronoun Has a Specific Antecedent (22b)

Pronoun references in the following sentences are vague. Read each sentence carefully and correct any problems either by inserting words where needed or rewriting the entire sentence.

1. My mother never graduated from college and works as a volunteer at Good Samaritan Hospital; this is what is so depressing to her.

2. Gert gave the message to Donna before she left for the day.

3. Pedro owned bowling shoes although he didn't do it often.

4. In movies, they often expect us to believe the most improbably events.

5. If you see Laura and her sister, will you make sure she knows that the party has been postponed?

6. My sister is now a well-known mathematician, which she got a D in when she was in high school.

7. I read in the paper that hospital costs are going up, and this started an argument between my brother and me.

8. The book was lying on the table, and it was soaking wet.

9. I bought a leather purse because it lasts longer than vinyl.

10. Rick asked Herb about his pet anaconda.

11. When he was crying, I became upset. This was why no one answered the phone when you called.

12. I used to want to be an accountant, but I got a C in it, so I changed my mind.

13. Each cashier is assigned a bagger for her work period, but they have been unable to keep up with the increased flow of customers.

14. I didn't realize that Ben had not read your letter before he called you. This is what caused all the trouble.

15. Kate explained to Marie that she had not done the correct assignment.

16. In the *New York Times*, they say that there is too much vocationalism in higher education.

17. The parents told their boys they would have to spend some time cleaning their room.

18. She graduated and joined the navy, which surprised me greatly.

19. The year George taught a course with Dennis, he did most of the work.

20. I took your pants to be cleaned, it's on my way to school.

# Exercise 23-1: Basic Pronoun Agreement (23a)

Correct any errors in the following sentences. All errors involve pronoun agreement. Each sentence may contain no errors, one error, or more than one error.

1. The voter should make sure their registration is up to date each year.

2. When a person tells one lie, sooner or later they will need to tell another.

3. A student should take their writing courses early because good writing will help them in most of their other courses.

4. You must have confidence in what your spouse is doing when they are not with you.

5. When a telephone rings, not many people can avoid answering them.

6. The police officer should make sure their uniform is always spotless.

7. Nurses often feel compassion for their patients.

8. A cat often sharpens their claws on the furniture.

9. When a gardener purchases a lot of bulbs, they expect that most of them will actually come up the following spring.

10. A newspaper reporter should have their questions written down before they start to interview someone.

# Exercise 23-2:
# Pronoun Agreement with Compound Antecedents (23c), with Indefinite Pronoun Antecedents (23d) and with Collective Noun Antecedents (23e)

Correct any errors in the following sentences. Each sentence may contain no errors, one error, or more than one error.

1. A cardinal or a blue jay can be easily identified by the crest on top of their heads.

2. Joyce or Fran will lend you her umbrella.

3. Ken or Kevin was flexing his muscles.

4. The teacher or the students will have to compromise his principles.

5. Either the cabinet officers or the President will place their initials on the document.

6. If you buy avocados or tomatoes, make sure it is ripe.

7. The bishops and the cardinals were making their flight reservations with Pan Am.

8. Massachusetts or Michigan cast their electoral votes for Ross Perot.

9. Everybody should bring their lunches on the bus; we will supply soft drinks.

10. Each of the contestants performed their act in three minutes.

11. Both of the horses tossed its head to the music.

12. Someone should donate his or her guitar to the band.

13. Has anyone seen an orange cat lurking around their house in the past three days?

14. The student who works hard in her course will raise their average considerably.

15. Half of the children saved their money.

16. The garden really shows their colors in the spring.

17. The committee asked itself if it was doing the right thing.

18. The association gave their highest award to Paul.

19. The team signed its autographs on the game ball.

20.  The bicycle group knows that the amount of fun it will have depends

upon the weather.

## 23-3:  Review of Pronoun Agreement

The following sentences contain errors involving pronoun reference or agreement.
Read each sentence carefully and correct any errors.  To correct some of the
errors, it may be necessary to rewrite the sentence completely.

1.  The sky was beginning to get darker, and I had missed the last bus to
    Washington.  This was making me very worried.

2.  Kathy smiled at Audrey, but she looked very solemn when I saw her.

3.  My friend Joe gave me a squash racket even though I had never played it
    in my life.

4.  Each of the waiters checked their table assignments before leaving for
    the kitchen.

5.  Donna and her parents showed me their new condominium.

6.  Someone left their umbrella at my apartment.

7.   Either Victor or Stanley will lend you his car.

8.   I got my resume typed on a word processor, and after three interviews, I was hired as a data processor for the Social Security Administration. I really appreciated Maxine's help with this.

9.   After Ralph gave Marc the letter from Gloria, he turned and walked away without saying a word.

10.  Each of the candidates must do their own work.

11.  When Kirby or Ned raises their hand, I know the class is in for a big laugh.

12.  Each of the guests brought a plant with them.

13.  Either the players or the coach will have to be more reasonable about his demands.

14. Most of the children could not even write his or her name.


15. I bought these shoes at Ward's during the spring sale. This is why they are so cheap.


# Exercise 24-1:
# Pronoun Case Errors: Subjects vs. Objects (24a), Case After Linking Verbs (24b), and Case in Compound Structures (24c)

Correct any errors in the following sentences. All errors will involve pronoun case. Each sentence may have no errors, one error, or more than one error.

1. Janine's children looked toward she for guidance.


2. Who's book is that on the table?


3. Just between you and I, this class does not relate to the real world.


4. Somebody left they're book on the table.


5. Please return those pencils to them who loaned they to you.


6. It became clear to she that the work would be a little harder than she had expected.


7. Kevin admitted that it was him who had left the computer on all night.

8.   This project will be shared by we and they.

9.   It was me who called you last night.

10.  Ernesto and her talked things over calmly.


# Exercise 24-2:
# Pronoun Case Errors with Appositives (24d) and with *We* and *Us* Before Nouns (24e)

Correct any errors in the following sentences. All errors will involve pronoun case. Each sentence may have no errors, one error, or more than one error.

1.   Us students know how to get pronoun case right.

2.   My cat vomited on her favorite person in the whole world, I.

3.   The teacher kept glowering at the group of students he thought was making the noise, us.

4.   Maybe us citizens should remember that we elected this president.

5.   If you ask we writers, you will find out how much work it takes to write well.

6.   Even the two best students, Ling and her, couldn't understand the homework last night.

7.   I am writing because us customers are getting tired of the sloppy repair jobs you do on our cars.

8.   If you cooperate during the interview with we reporters for the school paper, you will get good coverage.

9. The originators of this proposal, Juan and me, would like to be rewarded for our efforts.

10. We sophomores are not used to this kind of treatment.

# Exercise 24-3:
# Pronoun Case Errors with *Than* and *As* (24f) and *Who* and *Whom* (24g)

Correct any errors in the following sentences. All errors will involve pronoun case. Each sentence may have no errors, one error, or more than one error.

1. Almost everyone is a better speller than me.

2. Herb listens to music more intently than me.

3. Billy can type as fast as he.

4. As far as I can tell, you are as good at math as her.

5. To who does this mitten belong?

6. My mother likes Sylvia better than she.

7. A student who I haven't seen in a while came to see me today.

8. The letter was addressed to "who it may concern."

9.   A doctor who Darlene respects greatly came to talk to her class.

10.   Doris went to see her grandparents, with whom she enjoys talking.

# Exercise 24-4: Review of Pronoun Case Errors (24a-g)

Correct any errors in the following paragraph. All errors will involve pronoun case.

Peter just received a phone call from a supervisor at a park out west about a position as a volunteer ranger this summer. Peter told the supervisor that it was him who had called earlier to inquire about a position. The supervisor, whom sounded quite friendly, said they did need help. Peter said that a friend with who he had spoken earlier had told him that the work was extremely rigorous. The supervisor said that volunteers whom were in good shape would not have any trouble. Peter next asked, "Will us volunteers work six days a week?" The supervisor said yes, but that they would work only half days on Saturdays and Mondays. He had interviewed the volunteers from the previous summer, and, according to they, the job was challenging but rewarding. He urged Peter to send the application back to they as soon as possible.

# Exercise 25-1:
# Errors with Form of Irregular Verbs (25b)

Correct any errors in the following sentences. Each sentence may contain no errors, one error, or more than one error.

1. My mother has leaved for Tucson without her suitcase.

2. Mr. Alzamora has been sick for a week.

3. Roosevelt had brung a llama to his senior prom.

4. Kent has slud safely into third base, but the other team has protested.

5. My cat has hurt her paw.

6. Bob said that he had gave at the office.

7. My parents have sang in the Handel Choir for ten years.

8. Jim has broke Debbie's heart.

9. The school has bended the rules, and she knew it.

10. Have you ate yet?

11. Joseph has not wore the new tie I gave him.

12. Perhaps I should not have chose a purple tie with pink roses on it.

13. Prices have went so high that I have to quit school.

14. I think they have hit an all time high.

15. My father has ran his business the same way for thirty years.

16. I hate Linda Sadler, and I have feeled that way for a long time.

17. I have wrote a letter, but she has not wrote back.

18. These irregular verbs have drove me crazy.

19. In addition, they have thrown me for a loop.

20. I will probably have trouble with these until hell has freezed over.

## Exercise 25-2: Errors with Form of *Lie* and *Lay* (25d) and Omitted *-ed* (25f)

Correct any errors in the following sentences. All errors will involve verb forms. Each sentence may have no errors, one error, or more than one error.

1. My cat lays around the house all day.

2. You're suppose to come to a complete stop before proceeding through that intersection.

3. If you lie the parts out first, it will be easier to see how to assemble them.

4. Rick use to run much faster than he does now.

5. Brian laid down for a little nap before dinner.

6. That darn cat has laid on the couch all afternoon.

7.    Before I lain my wallet on the dresser, I checked to see how much money I had.

8.    Every time that happen, I found myself getting depressed.

9.    He ask if he was playing his stereo too loudly.

10.   Last night she fix me a glass of orange juice when we got home.

# Exercise 26-1:
# Finding and Revising Errors with Verb Tense (26a-d)

Correct any errors in the following sentences. All errors will involve verb tense. Each sentence may have no errors, one error, or more than one error.

1.    I lived at this address for the past ten years.

2.    Before she moved to Stockton, Melia has lived in Japan.

3.    Dan worked diligently on his model train for ten years, when he heard about the local model train club.

4.    Carol Friedman lived in Manhattan for ten years, but now she is moving to New Jersey.

5.    Since I waited for thirty minutes, I left without Tonya.

6.    Rose Torres handed me a note and runs back into the bedroom.

7.    We warmed up for fifteen minutes, so now we can start aerobics.

8.    Chuck was waiting for two hours when Carla finally showed up.

9.   I ate dinner, but I would love a cup of coffee.

10.  Lance was on the committee for three years, so they asked him to be the chair.

11.  Last week my mother help me fix the carburetor on my Chevy.

12.  By the time we get to the movie, it will be showing for a half hour.

13.  At the rate we are driving, the auction will be going on for an hour when we get there.

14.  Paul stands up and yelled for his dog.

15.  In July, Maria and her husband will be married for six years.

# Exercise 26-2: Finding and Revising Errors with Verb Tense (26e-g)

Correct any errors in the following sentences. All errors will involve the use of progressive verb forms or of active or passive voice. Each sentence may have no errors, one error, or more than one error.

1.   Right now, Henry takes a nap.

2.   I predict that when we get to Jeanine's apartment, she will read the homework for tomorrow.

3.   The car that was driven by Harry had been parked next to the police station.

4.   More than likely, Joe will work in his garden as we arrive.

5.   It was made clear to Noriko by Sheila that no more delays would be tolerated.

6.   A large tip was given by the customer who had been rude to the waitress.

7.   I just thought about Leslie as the phone rang.

8.   As I cooked dinner last night, I realized the dog barked for at least five minutes.

9. A mistake was made by my math professor, and none of us even noticed.

10. A raise of $1200 was given to Rosita by her boss.

# Exercise 28-1:
# Distinguishing Between Adjectives and Adverbs (28a-b)

Correct the errors in the following sentences. All errors will involve confusion between adjectives and adverbs. Each sentence may have no errors, one error, or more than one error.

1. My neighbor pulled careful out of the driveway.

2. Tawanda felt badly about canceling the party, but she really had no choice.

3. Angie is a very carefully driver most of the time.

4. Jennifer opened the door slow and looked around the empty auditorium.

5. The teacher sounded angrily when he called me last night.

6. Don't speak too fastly when you are delivering your speech.

7. Dave snored so loud that he woke his whole family.

8. Vergie sings quite good and will probably get a part in the play.

9. The Dean looked angry when we met with her.

10. My dog smells badly, so he is useless for hunting.

# Exercise 28-2:
# Comparative and Superlative Forms (28c)

Correct the comparative and superlatives in these sentences.

1. Henry is more kinder to us now that a little time has passed.

2. Kris was beautifuler in her new dress.

3. Between my road bike and my mountain bike, I like my mountain bike the mostest.

4. Lemons are more tangier than limes.

5. The beach is more better if you bring good music along with you.

6. It was the littlest number of stars in the sky I had seen.

7. James performed as badly as he ever has; it was worst than the time he had taken flu medicine and couldn't think straight.

# Exercise 28-3: Avoiding Double Negatives (28d)

Proofread the following sentences and correct any errors.

1.  It does not do no good to try to cool the house with the refrigerator door open.

2.  It's not unusual for it to rain here for several days in a row.

3.  I can't help but ask if the semester will ever end.

4.  I didn't do nothing.

5.  Misty, Julie's dog, seldom never comes inside when she calls her.

# Exercise 29-1: A vs. An (29a)

Proofread the following sentences and correct any errors. Each sentence may contain no errors, one error, or more than one error.

1.  Sheree doesn't know how to play an ukulele, even though she is supposed to.

2.  In the refrigerator, you can find an orange or an grapefruit.

3. We're looking for an yellow sweater with blue stripes.

4. A orangutan is a lot smaller than a gorilla.

5. We just passed a couple on a bicycle built for two.

6. Do you know an good Italian restaurant?

7. The movie was about the effects of a atomic bomb.

8. An elephant is not larger than a whale.

2.  AAA is great when you have minor problems.  Such as a flat tire, a dead battery or an overheated engine.  I recommend that you become a member.

3.  Brenda has ignored me at the last three meetings.  Also, she didn't invite me to her wedding.  Now, I am going to get even with her.

4.  I drove my car without any water in the radiator.  As a result, cracking the engine block.  The bill will be more than $500.

5.  My insurance company paid my claim within two weeks of the accident.  Plus, they rented a car for me while mine was being repaired.

6. The plane was thirty minutes late. Therefore, we missed our connecting flight in Chicago. As a result we didn't get home until three in the morning.

7. My brother has done many foolish things. Such as getting married four times. Also, he has quit at least seven jobs.

8. Several people have helped Janice get where she is today. For instance, the teacher who encouraged her to play the piano. Also, she was greatly assisted by her brother, who is a fine musician himself.

9. The management at my apartment building really takes care of things. Such as the time that my furnace quit in the middle of a snowstorm. The plumber was there fifteen minutes after I called and had it fixed an hour later.

10. My life is filled with unpleasant tasks these days. For example, I have to get up at six every morning. Also, on Thursdays I have to go grocery shopping after a full day at work.

# 32-4: Avoiding Comma Splices (32c)

Correct any errors in the following sentences. All errors are comma splices.

1. At first I loved my job, now I hate it.

2. I would love a glass of ice water, my mouth is dry.

3. As I walked into the bank, I noticed it was unusually quiet.

4. My boss just quit, he is moving to Houston.

5. When Marcy called last night, I was not very coherent, it was three o'clock in the morning.

6. Until I hear from Danali, I am not writing her another letter.

7. If it snows on Friday, we will have to cancel the meeting.

8. Ms. Macrae's job is exciting, she is a reporter for Channel 11.

9. Michelle's dress doesn't fit her right, it belongs to her sister.

10. Eugene's cake was terrible, he forgot the eggs.

# 32-5: Avoiding Run-ons (32c)

Correct any fused sentences in the following items. If the sentence is correct, do not make any change.

1. I gave the book to Wayne he had lent it to me three weeks ago.

2. These marbles are valuable they are more than one hundred years old.

3. Hondas are great cars they hardly ever need repairs.

4. My father grew up in a small town in Georgia. Hortense still does not have any traffic lights.

5. Sheila does a lot of traveling and never complains about it.

6. Alexis is moving to New York she found a great job.

7. The homework in psychology is hard we have to design a pure experiment.

8. Ms. Hesler walked into the room and handed back the papers.

9. I'm going to visit an old aunt of mine. She lives in San Diego.

10. Dave Berry did well in his chemistry course he likes doing experiments.

# Exercise 32-6:
# Review of Avoiding Fragments, Run-ons, and Comma Splices

The following selection contains fragments, run-on sentences, and comma splices. Reading the passage the passage carefully and correct any errors.

Work is a hard word to define, it has too many different meanings. It seems to mean anything that requires an expenditure of energy. Like carrying furniture or unloading ships. However, some kinds of work don't involve expending energy I'm thinking of computer programming or accounting. Unless you count mental energy. On the other hand, some activities that expend a lot of energy are not really work. Playing tennis takes a lot of energy. Especially the way I play. However, it's not considered work. Maybe work is anything you get paid for doing. That would cover computer programming and accounting, and it would not include tennis. However, it also would not include chopping wood or shoveling snow. Which both seem like a lot of work to me. It also would include winning the lottery or inheriting a million dollars neither of these is really work.

# Exercise 33-1:
# Using Commas and Coordinating Conjunctions to Join Independent Clauses (33a)

Correct any errors in the following sentences. All errors involve using commas and coordinating conjunctions. Each sentence may contain no errors, one error, or more than one error.

1.    George got contact lenses and grew a beard.

2.    I can write my paper on Friday or I can stay home on Sunday and do it.

3.    Stan likes seafood but he hates lobster.

4.    Theresa will fix dinner for all of us, or we can go out to Milano's.

5.    The flu always makes me feel exhausted, and gives me a headache.

6.    We will put our furniture in storage, and sell the house.

7.    Linda is not going to the bar with us for she is only sixteen.

8.    An airplane flew low over the stadium, and dropped leaflets on the crowd.

9.    We opened the door and yelled for Champ but he did not come.

10.    I had not ordered a pizza but the manager at Domino's insisted that I had.

# Exercise 33-2:
# Using Semicolons to Join Independent Clauses (33b)

Correct any errors in the following sentences. All errors involve comma splices or run-on sentences. Use semicolons to correct these errors.

1. My car is in the repair shop, the brakes are being relined.

2. I loved the movie last night it was about my hometown.

3. There is one thing that really makes me angry; a man who doesn't respect women.

4. Give me a call when you arrive in Chicago.

5. This book is extremely old, it was written in the eighteenth century.

6. My child has had all the common childhood diseases; like mumps, measles, and chicken pox.

7. Jack is not going to the dance, he has to work at the sub shop.

8. Juanita can take care of that cut; because she used to be a nurse.

9. I can't open the wine I don't have a corkscrew.

10. This has been a terrible day I lost my purse on the bus.

# Exercise 33-3:
# Punctuating Sentences with Conjunctive Adverbs (33c)

Proofread the following sentences carefully and correct any errors in punctuating independent clauses. Each sentence may contain no errors, one error, or more than one error.

1. Leslie charms everyone she meets, therefore, I am happy that I met her.

2. I had already seen the movie; however, I didn't mind seeing it again.

3. My hometown was sleepy and quiet, for example; we had only one stop light.

4. Rita forgot her umbrella, as a result, she got completely soaked.

5. My brother likes unusual sports; for example, rugby, squash, and water polo.

6. The food is much better at the Stone Inn; also there is plenty of parking.

7. We hoped that Margie would win the tournament; yet, we knew she didn't have much of a chance.

8. The new apartment had two bathrooms, as a result; we could all sleep fifteen minutes later in the mornings.

9. Kwok had two flat tires yesterday, in addition, he did not have a spare.

10. Gerry put away the groceries; meanwhile, Nancy made a salad.

11. I want to go to New York this summer; but, I don't have the money.

12. We ordered a spinach salad, instead the waiter brought us spinach pie.

13. The war had started. Therefore most young men had to change their career plans.

14. The parking lot was full, consequently we parked across the street.

15. Most mushrooms are harmless, still some can make you sick.

# Exercise 33-4:
# Punctuating Compound Complex Sentences (33d)

Correct any errors in the following. All errors will involve punctuation of compound complex sentences. Each item may involve no errors, one error or more than one error.

1. After the long winter everyone thought springtime would never come for the cold weather just wouldn't go away.

2. But then a warm spell arrived and it seemed like there was no stopping Mother Nature after that.

3.   It was initially difficult for people to believe that a tree could have so many leaves especially after seeing them so barren for so long yet it soon became difficult to imagine a tree without thousands of leaves.

4.   Many people were relieved to see the plants doing so well since ice storms during the winter had been so damaging

5.   Indeed some trees were left with only a limb or two which made them look somewhat forlorn but they were full of bright, green leaves.

# Exercise 33-5:
# Review of Using Commas and Semicolons to Punctuate Independent Clauses

Correct the following sentences. Each sentence below contains at least one comma punctuation error.

1.   Karen went to the grocery store, and then forgot what she wanted to buy so she just wandered the aisles for a while.

2.   I'll be on the East Coast for a few days next month, consequently, I might drop in and see you.

3.  Almost all of the commissioners attended the meeting, one, though, was sick.

4.  Julie had studied hard and knew the material, however, she was not good at taking tests under pressure.

5.  David cleaned the stove, counter, and floor and he washed the dishes.

6.  Nothing happened when I mixed the chemicals together, therefore, my experiment was a failure.

7.  Stu decided to go to bed early for it had been a long day.

8.  When I looked out the window an hour later the kids were still playing their games and the parents remained nearby.

9.  The dinner was delicious when everything was finally ready yet Marcy was still hungry afterward.

10. We went to a matinee so we could save on the admission price.

# Exercise 34-1:
# Using Commas with Introductory Elements (34a)

Correct any errors in the following sentences. Each sentence may contain no errors, one error, or more than one error.

1.  While she was playing a Beethoven sonata she got a cramp in her hand.


2.  To join the Jaycees he had to pay a lot of money.


3.  Organizing a girl Scout troop was more demanding than she thought.


4.  While she was looking carefully in the ditch. She spotted the wounded quail.


5.  Opening the envelope, Barb became excited.


6.  Checking the dictionary is the only way to be sure about spelling.


7.  In spite of my doubts about his discretion. He did not tell Marcy about the rumors.

8. To get a camping spot on the fourth of July. Is almost impossible in Yosemite.

9. To get commas in the right places you have to understand everything about sentences.

10. To be accepted to the Naval Academy was quite an honor.

11. As she gave me a knowing look. She answered the phone.

12. Looking down I didn't see Joanie. She was just getting home from her trip.

13. Because he objected to Vivian's comments. Brian stormed out of the room.

14. To my way of thinking we should invite the entire class to the party.

15. While the potatoes boil for half an hour. You can mix the ingredients for the topping.

# Exercise 34-2:
# Using Commas with Items in a Series (34b)

Correct the errors in the following sentences. Each sentence may contain no errors, one error, or more than one error.

1.  If you are going to the Safeway, would you get milk Cheerios and sugar?

2.  Debbie, Linda, and Theresa, are going to California for the summer.

3.  Mike served, sandwiches, potato salad, coleslaw, and iced tea for lunch.

4.  Leslie put mothballs in her suitcases in her closet and in her footlocker.

5.  I expected Randy and Howard to help me with the deliveries.

6.  Airlines, trains, and buses, were delayed by this weekend's snowstorm.

7.  The salad contained spinach lettuce cabbage cucumbers and tomatoes.

8.  I found sand in my pockets in my purse and in my ears when I got back from the beach.

9. Tom's car chokes, coughs, and sputters when it first starts, but it always runs fine once it is warmed up.

10. The high jump the discus throw and the pole vault are my favorite events in the Olympics.

# Exercise 34-3:
# Using Commas with Restrictive and Non-restrictive Clauses, Phrases, and Appositives (34c)

Some of the sentences below are correctly punctuated and others aren't; correct the ones that aren't.

1. That tree a cherry tree will produce some great-tasting berries in a couple of months.

2. College students, who often put more energy into partying than studying, sometimes regret that they didn't work harder.

3. The birds, where I live, begin their loud singing before sunrise sometimes.

4. Fireworks, exploding overhead, is an entrancing sight.

5.    Her letter a long and thoughtful discourse on "ninety-nine ways to fix

      spaghetti" made me laugh.


6.    People who chew their food with their mouths open drive Pat crazy.


7.    Jill's new job, a big opportunity for her, is also a lot of fun.


8.    The outfielder running hard to her right made an outstanding

      backhanded catch.


9.    Dickens' novel in which Pip learns the value of friendship is one of his

      finest.


10.   That book *Great Expectations* has been a favorite for more than 100

      years.


# Exercise 34-4:
# Using Commas to Set Off Parenthetical Expressions, Nouns of Direct Address, Yes and No, Interjections, and Tag Questions (34d)

Correct any errors in the following sentences.  All errors will involve commas. Each sentence my contain no errors, one error, or more than one error.

1.  That's a good idea if you ask me.

2.  Mr. Speaker will you let me have the floor?

3.  Yes I saw several shooting stars last night.

4.  That's a dangling modifier isn't it?

5.  Oh did you see how that cat just missed being hit by that car?

6.  Well don't look at me.  I didn't leave the light on all night.

7.  It's not true that George Washington actually chopped down a cherry tree is it?

8.  She's a good dog in my opinion as long as you give her enough exercise.

9.  I've been a good boy all year long Santa so I deserve a lot of presents.

10. Yes I'll help you mow the grass even though I'm busy right now.

# Exercise 34-5:
# Using Commas with Coordinate and Cumulative Adjectives (34e) and Absolute Phrases (34f)

The sentences below either contain unnecessary commas or they need commas; identify the problem and fix it.

1.  The bright sunny day made everyone feel happy after all the recent rain.

2.  Monica loves her new lightweight, cordless phone.

3.  We saw a herd of big, noisy, buffalo during our trip through Yellowstone National Park.

4.  Barbara's stubborn old horse would not come down to the barn.

5.  People up here know how important it is to have full-treaded, snowtires on their cars in the winter.

6.  It having rained earlier the air was humid.

7.  Simon sat down to read his work done for the day.

8. The test was more difficult than she expected, so Sherry wanting to get a good grade in the class decided she would study more.

9. The pie cooked and cooled sat ready for Susan to come home and eat it.

10. The trip extensively researched and planned turned out well.

# Exercise 34-6:
# Using Commas with Contrasted Elements (34g) and with Quotations (34h)

The sentences below either contain unnecessary commas or they need commas; identify the problem and fix it.

1. Her recipe explicitly calls for one tablespoon not two of nutmeg.

2. Unlike the maples the sycamores held up fairly well in the storm.

3. Van Gogh was a post-impressionist not an impressionist.

4. The car I have now unlike my previous one drives well.

5.   All of Michelle's classes but one are going well this semester.

6.   "I think the council does not listen to the people" she told the reporter.

7.   The reporter asked "Why do you say that?"

8.   "Because they don't care what people think" she said.  "They're going to do what they want no matter what."

9.   The reporter then asked "Can you point toward a specific example?"

10.  "The commission's vote two weeks ago" she said "is an example."

# Exercise 34-7:
# Using Commas with Dates and Places (34i)

Correct the errors in the following sentences.  Each sentence may contain no errors, one error, or more than one error.

1.   My accident occurred on Friday June 27, 1989 at ten o'clock in the evening.

2.   The Allied Company has asked for a delivery date in November, 1993.

3.  My first daughter was born in Colorado Springs Colorado on Wednesday October 11 1966.

4.  Lenny, Marc, and Bill were all hired on 30 August 1989.

5.  January 25 1994 is the deadline for applying for these benefits.

6.  Clifford Still began work on this painting in May 1981 and completed it in August of that year.

7.  I lived in Kansas City Missouri until October 1 1988.

8.  Do you know what happened on December 7 1941?

9.  The meeting I missed was scheduled for Thursday April 16 1992 instead of Thursday April 23.

10. As of 1 January 1995 I will never make another error.

# Exercise 34-8:
# Review of Comma Rules (32c, 33a, and 34)

Correct the errors in the following sentences. All errors will involve comma use, including comma splices and commas used with coordinating conjunctions to join independent clauses. Each sentence may have no errors, one error, or more than one error.

1. Santos joined the army on October 12 1994 at two o'clock in the afternoon.

2. Gino wrote a paper on computerized reservation systems for hotels, he is studying to be a computer programmer.

3. If I were you, Aaron I would not go to Quincey's party.

4. I can't go with you to the movies for I am completely out of cash.

5. This book is too difficult, it is full of technical medical jargon.

6. Lara, Gary, and Jim, are working together on their papers this weekend.

7. To get an A from Professor Baldwin-Crane is not easy.

8. My father who works for a bakery is bringing two loaves of olive bread a pie and a cake to the party tonight.

9. Because of the snowstorm on Thursday night this college in my opinion should not have opened on Friday.

10. Maurice stood up suddenly, and hit his head on the bookshelf.

11. That small, green car belongs to Cheryl's grandfather.

12. Denine brought a wet, exhausted dog into the house last night.

13. When Bernie got to work, and found the door unlocked he called the police.

14. You can write to the museum at 11308, South Rim Road, Omaha, Nebraska, 58902.

15. If Dawn is free Friday morning we could have our meeting then.

16. The man, who gave me a ride to work this morning, was a friend of my music teacher.

17. Annette looked into my eyes and told me I was a great fool.

18. Corey fixed Eva a cup of coffee, and a bagel for breakfast.

19. Kansas City Missouri is larger than Kansas City Kansas.

20. Maeshon is quite angry with Andy, he forgot her birthday last week.

# Exercise 35-1:
# Forming Possessive Nouns (35a)

Read each of the following sentences and correct any errors. Each sentence may contain no errors, one error, or more than one error.

1.    The childrens screams could be heard all over the neighborhood.

2.    Several teachers were eating lunch in the student union.

3.    My cars' tires are low on air so I am driving it to a gas station.

4.    The Presidents' speech to Congress was misleading.

5.    In the evening's Darrell works at Gino's.

6.    Several police officers cars were vandalized.

7.    Six childrens' jackets were stolen from this department over the weekend.

8.    The players union did not agree to negotiate around the clock.

9.    Todays economy makes it necessary that peoples budgets be rigid.

10.   Can you tell me where the womens room is located?

11.   These doctors offices are too crowded.

12.   The two deers antlers became locked during their battle.

13.   The chairpersons' absence caused us to cancel the meeting.

14.   Nelson was awakened by sixty sheeps bleating.

15.   My bikes tires are easy to patch.

# Exercise 35-2:  Contractions (35c)

Proofread the following sentences and correct any errors.  Each sentence may contain no errors, one error, or more than one error.

1.    Theres no reason for you to fell embarrassed.

2.    My essay is'nt finished, but Im no worried about it.

3. Larry couldn't see why we were angry.

4. My sister wo'nt let me open doors for her.

5. Has'nt the bus stopped running on this street.

6. I wonder what they're going to do when their daughter does'nt come home from college for the summer.

7. Havent you read the morning paper yet?

8. I dont like asparagus.

9. Jazz is'nt for everyone, but I love it.

10. Whats for dinner tonight?

# Exercise 35-3:
# Confusion of Contractions and Possessives (35e)

Correct any errors in the following sentences. All errors will involve confusion of contractions and possessives with pronouns. Each sentence may have no errors, one error, or more than one error.

1. Their looking for oil in Virginia, but its unlikely they will find any.

2. I got my application in the mail, but Marlene hasn't gotten her's.

3. Its' too late to go swimming.

4. I hear your going to San Francisco this weekend.

5. I don't like they're attitude.

6. Tony's dog hurt its' leg, but its better now.

7. Michael isn't going to flunk his' accounting course, is he?

8. It's a shame that the election is being held so early.

9. There giving tickets to illegally parked cars this afternoon.

10. I don't know anyone whose going to the dance.

# Exercise 35-4:  Review of Apostrophes (35)

Proofread the following essay and correct any errors.  All errors involve the use of apostrophes.

Just once in my life, I would like to take an extreme position.  However, on every issue I can think of, I end up in the middle of the road.  I have come to the conclusion that I am compulsively moderate.

Take, for example, the matter of dress. My childrens clothes are interchangeable with those of their friends. There is'nt an ounce of individuality in anything they wear. I dont like that kind of conformity, but I also dont approve of my friend who tries to shock everyone by wearing the most bizarre outfits she can contrive. She's always showing up wearing large floppy hats, long feather earrings, and transparent blouses. You can see from this that my preference is for clothes that express individuality without being too extreme. And that is the problem: I never do anything extreme.

At my job I disapprove of people who can only say "yes" to the boss. I think people should have the courage to express they're opinions even when those opinions are different from the boss's. On the other hand, there are two men at work who seem to disagree with everything our boss says. They waste everyones time by objecting to every decision. They're negative attitudes are disruptive. So once again, I approve of a little rebelliousness, but not too much.

Nothing can ruin a visit to someones house more quickly than unruly children. Todays parents are often overly permissive. Lenient parents' who let they're children interrupt conversations and annoy the guests bother me more than almost anything. I say "almost" because there is one thing that offends me even more: tyrannical parents. I hate to see parents who have turned they're children into robots who can say only "Yes, Ma'am" and "Thank you, Sir." Spending an evening in that kind of militaristic environment can leave me depressed for weeks. Its not that I object to discipline, but I object to an excess of it. Once again, I end up a moderate.

Of course, moderation is all right in it's place. My problem is that I am always moderate. I can never take an extreme position. You might say that Im extremely moderate, but, at least, that means I've found something that I'm extreme about.

# Exercise 36-1: Quotations (36)

Provide quotation and other punctuation marks in the following sentences.

1.  I enjoy living in a small town, said my roommate. I like being able to ride my bike anywhere.

2.  I'll be here when you get back he said.

    I won't be gone long she replied

    Well I might miss you anyway.

3.   I'm so busy I don't have time to sleep is how I started my letter to my Mom and Dad, Patrick told his Professor.

4.   While My Guitar Gently Weeps is one of Susan's cat's favorite Beatles songs.

5.   Many people have problems with their, there, and they're.

6.   The shower we just had was closer to a monsoon.

7.   One of the definitions of gadfly is a firebrand.

8.   One student said "Sometimes I can't remember if periods go inside of quotation marks or out"

9.   Aaron's art professor said "Some colors complement each other: red and green, for example;" Aaron replied with another example:  How about blue and orange?

10.  "What are some differences between Hemingway's style and Fiztgerald's" was the test question.

11.  Did John say "*Moby Dick* is great book?"

# Exercise 37-1:
# Colons, Ellipses, Parentheses, Brackets, Dashes and Slashes (37)

Correct any errors with punctuation in the following sentences.

1.  Two aspects of last night's lightning storm were scary; the thunder and the high winds.

2.  On the desk were: some envelopes, a pencil, and a coffee cup.

3.  In Bill's knapsack were the following. a lot of dirty laundry and some crushed crackers.

4.  "Each year, after the midwinter blizzards, there comes a night of thaw when the tinkle of dripping water is heard . . ." (Leopold, 3)

5.  Remember that it might rain tomorrow.  (And remember, too, that it might get chilly).

6.   Mark's mother called him and said that "(she) would arrive next Monday."

7.   The news was better than we expected.  A relief after our recent heartache.

8.   If you cannot-will not attend the meeting, please let me know.

# Part VIII
# EDITING:
# MECHANICS

## Exercise 38-1: Capitalization (38)

Proofread the following paragraph and correct any errors. All errors will involve capitalization.

I have an Uncle who seems to have figured out the secret to being happy. About twenty years ago, he was a Doctor making lots of money and working seventy hours a week. One day, he announced he was quitting his practice and living for himself from then on. When he had been in College, he had worked his way through school by renovating houses, mostly for his friends. Now that he has quit medicine, he had gone back to what he always enjoyed most—renovation. He works only about four days a week and takes a vacation for two months every Winter. Last year he flew to Florida and rented a sailboat. He and his Irish Setter just sailed East into the Ocean for a month and then sailed back for a month. Then he was ready to go back to his work with a fresh outlook. The combination of doing a job he loves and not working very hard seems to guarantee that he is always happy.

# Exercise 44-1:
# Editing for Spelling Errors (44b)

Read the following sentences carefully and correct any spelling errors. Each sentence may contain, no errors, one error, or more than one error.

1. I beleived my borther was speaking a foriegn language.

2. It never occured to me that I would recieve a grant.

3. Editting is the hardest part of writting for me.

4. I was loveing the play until the third act, which was too depressing.

5. Professor Delpit said the homework in her class would be managable, even for those working full time.

6. Sook Moon worryed so much that it was noticable to everyone.

7. I don't believe that one can increase one's hieght by taking protien supplements.

8. Tawanda couldn't conceive of someone being so mean.

9.   Oppening the door, Winton looked into the garage.

10.  Maria's new car does not get better milage than her old one.

# Exercise 44-2:
# Editing for Spelling Errors (44c)

Read the following sentences carefully and correct any spelling errors.  Each
sentence may contain, no errors, one error, or more than one error.

1.   I was the twelth juror selected for this case.

2.   Jackie had to get four innoculations for her trip.

3.   My mother is mor inteligent than my father.

4.   Consuela is not ready for mariage, but her boyfriend is.

5.   Even though I have been here for two years, I am still considered a
     sophmore.

6.   Can you appriciate the awkwardness of my position?

7.   It was crual of Donna to decieve her boy friend.

8.   We hope to develope a faster way to calculate the company's profits.

9.   My mother's behavior embarassed me at the dance performance.

10.   Jeremy did not intend to start a quarell.


# Exercise 44-3:
# Finding words in a Dictionary When You Don't Know How to Spell Them (44d)

The following are misspellings of actual but unusual words; the spellings do indicate how the word sounds.  We are using such unusual words to show you that it is possible to find most words in the dictionary, even ones you have never seen before.  For each word, list as many possible spellings as you can.  Then refer to a dictionary to find the actual spelling.

1.   phlinse:  to strip the blubber or skin for a whale, seal, or other animal.

possible spellings: _____   _____

_____   _____

_____   _____

_____   _____

_____   _____

_____   _____

actual spelling: _____

eylate:  in chemistry, pertaining to a heterocyclic ring containing a metal n attached to at least two non-metal ions.

sible spellings: _____   _____

_____   _____

_____   _____

_____   _____

_____   _____

_____   _____

actual spelling:            _____


3.  highpurmneesia:  unusually exact or vivid memory

    possible spellings:  _____   _____

                         _____   _____

                         _____   _____

                         _____   _____

                         _____   _____

    actual spelling:     _____


4.  encubus:  an evil spirit or a nightmare that visits women while they sleep.

    possible spellings:  _____   _____

                         _____   _____

                         _____   _____

                         _____   _____

_____   _____

actual spelling: _____

5. flocks: a plant with lance-shaped leaves and clusters of white red, or purple flowers.

possible spellings: _____   _____

_____   _____

_____   _____

_____   _____

_____   _____

_____   _____

actual spelling: _____

# Exercises 44-4:
# Editing for Spelling Errors (44f)

Read the following sentences carefully and correct any spelling errors. Each sentence may contain, no errors, one error, or more than one error.

1. There were three churchs in my home town.

2. Hank is on good terms with all three of his former wifes.

3. Three sheeps were crossing the road.

4. A connection between coffee and cancer was not established in either of our studys.

5. Larry and Neal moved two pianoes into the concert hall.

6. We found our kitten hiding under some bushs.

7. Lorena and Kerry helped themselfs to some dessert.

8. Several deers have been hit by cars on this road.

9. I don't understand why people bring radioes to the beach.

10. A bouquet of lilys was sitting on the mantle.

# Exercise 44-5: Review of Spelling (44a-f)

Read the following sentences carefully and correct any spelling errors. Each sentence may contain, no errors, one error, or more than one error.

1. Serendra does not wiegh as much as he used to.

2. Were you listenning when Ray Cisneros announced he was applying for the job?

3. We were truley moved by her apology.

4. I would never have time to read a dailie paper.

5. Amoung my problems is my difficulty with grammer.

6. Oliver usualy redicules people who make mistakes.

7. None of Virginia's classs meet until Febuary.

8. Tien tried to pursuade Martha to go to the movies with her.

9. We bought three tomatos at the market.

10. The begining of this exercise created a dellemma for me.

# ANSWER KEY

In this chapter you will find the even answers to the exercises in the text. In many cases there is more than one correct way to revise a sentence or answer a question; we have attempted to give the most frequent response. If your answer is different from ours and you are not sure whether it is correct talk to your instructor.

**Exercise 1-1: Audience and Purpose (1c)**

2. to get an interview
4. to avoid a fight about your not spending the summer with them
   to allow them to plan for your visit from May 25 to June 1
   to impress them with your initiative in getting the job
6. to reduce the number of people who ask you to help them to run the machine
   to avoid damage to the machine
   to show your boss how well organized you are

**2-1: Focusing: Subject and Thesis (2b)**

2. Lyndon Johnson's crucial mistake was to commit American troops to Vietnam.
4. Lee Harvey Oswald really assassinated President Kennedy.
6. Married couples must understand that hard work is necessary to make marriages last.
8. The Civil War was caused by economic competition between the North and South.
10. Doctors make too much money.

**Exercise 2-2: Focusing Subject and Thesis (2b)**

2. Smoking should be banned in public places.
4. The 55 mph speed limit saves thousands of lives each year.

**Exercise 3-1: Distinguishing between Generalizations and Evidence**

2. The main assertion in this paragraph is "It was a terrible morning." The evidence to support this assertion is quite solid and convincing.
   a. I overslept
   b. no shower

c. toast burned
d. no more toast
e. battery dead
f. hour late for work

4. The main assertion is, "The local news on Channel 4 is a joke." There are a number of statements following this assertion that might look like evidence:
   a. newscasters don't take it seriously
   b. hardly ever cover any hard news
   c. almost all sensationalism
   d. don't even understand the stories they are covering
   e. always ask the people they are interviewing dumb questions.
   f. I watch it only for laughs.
   However, if you look closely at these statements, you will see that they are all assertions. There is, in reality, not one piece of hard evidence to support any of these assertions. For example, the statement that newscasters don't take it seriously isn't evidence; it is an opinion. The writer doesn't provide any examples to back it up. Each of the statements is like that—just the writer's opinion rather than real evidence.

6. The main assertion is "This town is in better shape than it's been in the last twenty-five years." The evidence to support this assertion includes some data, but it is primarily "expert opinion," statements from the mayor, the police chief and the presidents of the Chamber of Commerce and of the PTA. This kind of expert opinion is often good support for your assertions, as it is here.
   a. Mayor Washington reports that the average income is at its highest level ever.

b. Unemployment is a 6.5%, the lowest since 1967.

c. Chief of Police Daniels has repeatedly observed that the crime rate is lower than at any time since 1962.

d. The president of the Chamber of Commerce has announced that this year will be the best business year the town has experienced in twenty years.

e. Sixteen new businesses have opened, and only two have gone out of business in the past twelve months.

f. The president of the PTA has good news. Our children's scores have gone up for three years in a row.

## Exercise 7-1:  The Paragraph as a Unit of Thought (7a and b)

In paragraph 2, you should have crossed out "Eliot wrote poetry in which he described modern society as a wasteland."

## Exercise 8-1:  Providing Transitions (8a)

Paragraph 2 is much more effective than paragraph 1. Paragraph 2 is much easier to read, it flows more smoothly, and it is easier to follow.

## Exercise 8-2:  Providing Transitions (8a)

2. as a result, consequently, thus, because of this, therefore, for this reason, hence

4. for example, as an illustration, for instance, to illustrate

## Exercise 9-1:  Avoiding Shifts in Tense (9a)

Looking for a prom dress with my daughter was quite an experience. She announced that the girls in her school had decided they would not wear "real" prom dresses. Then she tried to explain what they would wear, but I couldn't understand it. We went to a huge mall with four major department stores. After five hours, I had held up forty-one dresses and asked, "Would you like something like this?" And the answer was consistently "No." So we tried a fancy ladies' dress shop, but nothing there would do. After a break for dinner, we drove to last department store in town, but nothing there would do either. Finally, we stopped at one last dress shop, and there she found the dress she wanted. It was a white strapless dress with a lot of gauzy material around the bottom. I could not see how it was any different from a traditional prom dress, but I was so relieved to have found a dress that I did not say a word.

## Exercise 9-2 Avoiding Shifts in Person and Number (9b)

Paragraph 2

You will find using a word processor to be much easier than you think. You merely type your paper using the keyboard of the computer exactly like a typewriter. Then, you use various combinations of keys to make changes in your paper. You can move words around, erase words, and insert words with just the flick of a key. Once you have used a word processor you will never go back to an old-fashioned typewriter.

## Exercise 9-3:  Avoiding Shifts in Mood and Voice (9c and 9d)

Most people agree on the basics of car maintenance. For example, change your oil every 3,000 miles, and at the same time you should check your tire pressure and tread wear. Other fluids, such as anti-freeze, brake and transmission fluids, should be added if necessary. But don't stop there. Mechanics recommend that filters and belts are checked regularly. One garage owner said that if he was me, he wouldn't drive a car with dirty filters or squealing belts. Careful car owners also know to keep a maintenance record. A complete upkeep and repair log is jotted down there, a practice which helps them operate their vehicles more efficiently. Maintaining a car isn't difficult, as long as it is done conscientiously and consistently. It will extend your car's life, and your headaches may be decreased as well.

## Exercise 11-1:  Coordinating Equal Ideas (11a)

2. The air is wonderfully fresh, but I can't decide whether I should ride my bike or go for a hike.

4. Afterward, I'll probably read for while, or I'll listen to music.

### Exercise 11-2: Subordinating Less Important Ideas (11b)

2. Tawanda, who is wearing a red sweater, bought a new puppy.
4. Investigators, who spent six hours probing the wreckage, discovered oil-soaked rags in the basement.

### Exercise 12-1: Correcting Faulty Parallelism (12a-f)

2. This weekend we did some reading, went to a movie, and went to Tommy's party.
4. Julian's plan was to finish his research, write his note cards, and to complete a rough draft of his term paper by the first of March.
6. Students in this class are gaining confidence in themselves and enthusiasm for writing.
8. Having studied the piano for five years and she had sung having sung in her church choir since she was eight, so she had no trouble getting an A in Music 101.
10. So far in this class, we studied the Greeks, the Romans, and the Middle Ages.

### Exercise 13-1: Avoiding Misplaced Modifiers (13a-e)

2. Walking past the lake, I was happy to see spring finally made its appearance.
4. Arriving early at my office, I found the door was locked.
6. I can read in the car only if the road is smooth.
8. Running in the marathon, Melia sprained her ankle.
10. Searching through his pockets, Timothy begged the bus driver to wait a minute.

### Exercise 15-1: Avoiding Mixed and Incomplete Constructions (15 a-e)

2. The reason for the mistake was that Lonny didn't understand what you wanted him to do.
4. This book is designed to explain the rules of grammar.
6. I took a course which was more difficult than I realized.

8. Carl is more successful than anyone else from his high school.
10. Sending the application meant that I would soon be enrolled in a rehabilitation program.

### Exercise 16-1: Choosing Effective Words (16a)

2. Even though the driver applied her brakes gradually, the truck spun out of control.
4. If you hear anything new about the election, give me a call.
6. Julie's personal goals do not include having children.
8. When I passed that truck, the driver flashed his lights at me.
10. This job requires too much patience for me.

### Exercise 16-2: Choosing Effective Words (16a)

2. The effect of her decision is that we're going to get a new computer.
4. Donna is no better at swimming than John is.
6. Michael made up his mind and passed the reading course in one semester.
8. Except for Monday, the weather was really fine while we were at the Cape.
10. I would rather lose the contest than be thought of as a cheater.
12. Your advice had a good effect on Joan's attitude.
14. When the weather is hot, you should wear loose clothes.
16. She went to the personnel office to find out about her retirement benefits.
18. I didn't hear from the teacher, so I guess I passed the course.
20. I can't quite accept his explanation for his mistake; it's not like him.

### Exercise 16-3: Choosing Effective Words (16a)

2. I find that I like most foods once I get used to them.
4. We're worried about the effect this experience may have on her career.

6. We should <u>have</u> gone <u>to</u> a Chinese restaurant because Mary likes Chinese food much better then Italian.

8. Students are <u>supposed</u> <u>to</u> read a chapter of the text each week.

10. I think Joe could <u>have</u> <u>passed</u> this <u>course</u>, <u>except</u> for the statistics.

12. Troy <u>used</u> to live in Phoenix until he <u>quit</u> his job and moved back here.

14. Two dollars would <u>have</u> been enough for a tip; the <u>dessert</u> was terrible.

16. We didn't want to <u>lose</u> the game, but they <u>were</u> just <u>too</u> good for us.

18. Do you mine if Robin and Norm try <u>to</u> <u>find</u> her earring.

20. It is <u>all right</u> if they make fun of me; I'm <u>used</u> to it.

## Exercise 16-4: Choosing Effective Words (16a)

A few months later, he resigned <u>and</u> transferred <u>to</u> Virginia Tech. After a year there, he disappeared and, six months later, reappeared living in New York, married, and enrolled in Columbia. At Columbia he majored in English and got straight A's. I don't <u>know</u> <u>whether</u> it was New York, marriage, or Columbia, but something sure had a good <u>effect</u> on him.

## Exercise 19-1: Recognizing Nouns (19a)

2. Two <u>cardinals</u> flew into the <u>window</u> of my <u>living room</u>.

4. A <u>lunch</u> of <u>salad</u> and <u>soup</u> does not have many <u>calories</u>.

6. There are no nouns.

8. <u>Communication</u> is important to a good <u>relationship</u>.

10. Her <u>desk</u> is located in the <u>corner</u> of her <u>bedroom</u>.

## Exercise 19-2: Recognizing Pronouns (19b)

2. Carl was helping <u>himself</u> to the desserts.

4. Ruth gave <u>us</u> good advice.

6. Tim and Gail said <u>they</u> would be here by nine o'clock.

8. <u>Most</u> of the children don't believe in Santa Claus, but <u>many</u> of <u>them</u> pretend <u>that they</u> do.

10. <u>Half</u> of the children had colds, but <u>that</u> didn't slow <u>them</u> down.

## Exercise 19-3: Recognizing Verbs (19c)

Nathaniel Hawthorne's novel *The Scarlet Letter* <u>tells</u> the story of Hester Prynne. Hester <u>was</u> a young woman living in Boston in the colonial days of the Massachusetts Bay Colony. She <u>was married</u> to a much older scholar. Her husband <u>had</u> not yet <u>come</u> over from England. Despite her marriage, she <u>fell</u> in love with Arthur Dimmesdale, a popular minister in the Puritan church. She and Arthur <u>made</u> love once. Unfortunately, she <u>became</u> pregnant. In puritanical Boston, such behavior <u>was</u> both sinful and illegal. The church elders <u>demanded</u> the name of the father of Hester's child, but Hester <u>would</u> not <u>identify</u> him, and Dimmesdale <u>did</u> not <u>identify</u> himself. As a result, Hester <u>spent</u> a term in prison and <u>was</u> then <u>required</u> to wear a scarlet letter A on the breast of her dress for the rest of her life. On the day of her entry into prison, her husband <u>arrived</u> in Boston in disguise. He quickly <u>understood</u> the situation and fairly soon <u>identified</u> the father. He then <u>tormented</u> the remorseful and sickly Dimmesdale to the point of death. Finally, Dimmesdale <u>confessed</u> his sin at a public gathering and <u>died</u> on the spot. Hester <u>remained</u> in Boston and <u>converted</u> her scarlet letter into a symbol of honor and goodness, through her kindness to others, especially troubled women.

## Exercise 19-4: Distinguishing Verbs and Verbals (19c)

2. <u>Finding</u> a key in my purse <u>is</u> not easy.

4. To get a job, <u>Paul</u> <u>mailed</u> over one hundred resumes.

6. Looking to his left, <u>Kent</u> <u>did</u> not <u>notice</u> the approaching truck.

8. <u>To mail</u> that letter <u>will require</u> four stamps.

10. To raise tomatoes, <u>one</u> <u>must have</u> lots of sun.

12. Sitting at my typewriter, <u>I</u> <u>found</u> peace of mind.

14. <u>To reach</u> the ocean by noon <u>was</u> our plan.

16. <u>Holding</u> my head <u>made</u> my headache a lot better.

18. To teach her cat a lesson, <u>Helene</u> <u>tied</u> his paws together.

20. To cover his mistake, <u>Jeff</u> <u>had</u> to tell several lies.

## Exercise 19-5: Recognizing Parts of Speech (19d-g)

2. *adj.* <u>The</u> colors, *adj.* <u>multi-hued</u> and *adj.* <u>impressive</u>, *adv.* <u>quickly</u> filled *adj.* <u>the</u> *adj.* <u>western</u> sky.

4. *adv.* <u>Amazingly</u>, it *adv.* <u>completely</u> transformed *adj.* the *adv.* <u>somewhat</u> *adj.* <u>dejected</u> mood I had been experiencing.

6. Turn left <u>at</u> the second traffic light.

8. It's the one <u>across</u> the street <u>from</u> the pink house <u>with</u> blue shutters.

10. No prepositions.

12. *sub.* <u>Before</u> we can invite anyone else, we will need to check with Harriet to see if she can come *co-ord*

14. I will make a cake, <u>so</u> why don't you bring the ice cream.

## Exercise 20-1: Recognizing Subjects and Verbs (20 a-b)

2. <u>Joanne</u> and her <u>husband</u> <u>took</u> a trip to Wyoming and <u>saw</u> grizzly bears.

4. There <u>were</u> two <u>reasons</u> for her anger.

6. A <u>friend</u> of my sister <u>is</u> the president of CBS.

8. <u>Jim</u> and <u>Cathy</u> <u>will</u> not <u>be coming</u> to the meeting.

10. <u>Helen</u> and a <u>neighbor</u> of hers <u>will be</u> <u>waiting</u> for us at the station.

12. The <u>man</u> in the checked suit and the striped tie <u>is</u> my uncle.

14. My little <u>sister</u> and her <u>friend</u> <u>stayed</u> up late and <u>watched</u> television.

16. The <u>cover</u> of my typewriter <u>was lying</u> on the floor.

18. <u>Is</u> the <u>handle</u> of the lawn mower <u>broken</u>?

20. <u>One</u> of the boys and <u>none</u> of the girls <u>remembered</u> the name of the teacher.

## Exercise 20-2: Recognizing Parts of Sentences (20 c, d, e, i, and j)

2. Jeff's dog ate a <u>bone</u>.

4. The company received a phone <u>call</u> from an irate customer.

6. <u>In the library</u> are many books <u>about Thomas Jefferson</u>.

8. <u>Without a doubt</u>, the keys were <u>in the drawer</u> where I put them.

10. The cat <u>on that hot tin roof</u> is mine.

12. <u>Craig opened the door</u>, and <u>Nessie walked into the room wearing a large hat</u>.

14. <u>Maxine sat down at her computer and typed in the first line of her paper</u>.

16. <u>If you know the way</u>, I will ride with you.

18. <u>Because Julio took five courses and because he is very good at math</u>, he is getting straight A's this semester.

20. I gave my paper to the man <u>who is standing next to the window</u>.

## Exercise 21-1: Basic Subject-Verb Agreement (21a)

2. Teachers sometimes give a lot of homework on weekends.

4. My dog wakes me up every morning.

6. The supermarket charges more for the basics each week.

8. Often, the Murphy kids visit their grandparents.

10. These envelopes contain bonus checks for every employee.

12. The furnace at our apartment burns a lot of oil.

14. The baby seldom sleeps past seven in the morning.

16. That teacher gives low grades to most students.

18. The bank opens at 9:30 on Saturdays.

20. This stapler sometimes chews up the paper.

## Exercise 21-2: Subject-Verb Agreement with the Verb *to be* (21d)
2. The suspect's car is a late model Buick.
4. Marcy is living with her parents.
6. You are not welcome here.
8. I am surprised by the ending of the novel.
10. The students are angry with the dean.

## Exercise 21-3: Subject-Verb Agreement with Helping Verbs (21e)
2. My mother must worry a lot about my sister
4. That dog may be lost.
6. Ms. Caprio has opened a store.
8. Ford is bringing out new models in January.
10. My enemy would love to find out my plan.

## Exercise 21-4: Subject-Verb Agreement with Past and Future Tenses (21f)
Even though I will retire next May, the summer will be busy. My car is paid for, and my mortgage is paid off, so my expenses will be minimal. I will be working part time for a landscaping company, which means lots of sun, fresh air, and exercise. With my spare time, I will take a computer programming course at the local college. It will be wonderful to take a course just out of intellectual curiosity. I also will plant a good sized vegetable garden in my backyard. Besides all that, I will see every movie that comes to town.

## Exercise 21-5: Subject-Verb Agreement with Phrases that Come between Subject and Verb (21g), with Compound Subjects (21h), and with the Subject Following the Verb (21k)
2. The papers in this box belong to my grandmother.
4. The color of her eyes is a deep blue.
6. There are three choices for dessert.
8. Val's problem with languages is that she cannot remember vocabulary.
10. In the box are my good shoes.

12. A mouse or a rat is chewing the boxes in the basement.
14. The teacher or the students are going to apologize.

## Exercise 21-6: Subject-Verb Agreement with Indefinite Pronouns (21i), with Collective Nouns (21j), and with Linking Verbs (21l)
2. The crowd was impatient for the game to start.
4. Everyone of the students was studying for the exam.
6. A pair of kittens has taken over my life.
8. Either of the answers is correct.
10. Each of the books on the syllabus is more than three hundred pages long.
12. Everyone in my 8:00 class has been late at least once this semester.
14. Everybody that I know has already seen that movie.
16. A source of pollution that many people are not aware of is the many farms in the state.
18. My normal lunch these days is a couple of crackers.
20. The title of the book Mark chose to read was *Ten Ways to Lower Your Income Taxes*.

## Exercise 21-7: Subject-Verb Agreement in Clauses Beginning with *Who*, *Which*, or *That* (21m) and When the Subject is Plural in Form but Singular in Meaning (21n)
2. General Motors is laying off another six thousand employees.
4. Physics is extremely hard if you don't understand calculus.
6. Ten dollars were more than I expected for a tip from that table full of drunks.
8. The news from my wife's business is not very encouraging.
10. Four miles is long enough to walk on your first day back.

## Exercise 21-8: Review of Subject-Verb Agreement (21a-n)
Work is something most of us would like to avoid. As far back as Adam and Eve, work was seen as a curse, a punishment. Everyone I

know <u>loves</u> a day off from work. When a huge snowstorm or a power failure <u>causes</u> work to be canceled, everyone celebrates. Further, vacation time is an important part of the compensation we get for our jobs. Many of us <u>spend</u> our hard earned cash to buy "labor saving" devices, which <u>are</u> supposed to reduce the amount of work we do. It <u>does</u> seem that we <u>want</u> to avoid work.

There <u>are</u> many reasons why work is so important in our lives. For one thing, work often is what gives meaning to our lives. Work, when we are lucky, allows us to feel we are making some contribution to society. Through work, many of us gain a sense of success. Doing a job well makes us feel we are contributing to society.

Finally, we go to work because we would feel strange if we didn't. Going to work is what adults do in our society. In the past, this was true primarily for men, but today it has become true for most women as well. If we stay home from work on a weekday, anyone who <u>sees</u> us will assume we are sick. Going to work is normal.

### Exercise 22-1: Making Sure that a Pronoun Has One Clear Antecedent (22a) and Making Sure that a Pronoun Has a Specific Antecedent (22b)

2. Gert gave the message to Donna before Donna left for the day.
4. Movie directors often expect us to believe the most improbably events.
6. My sister is now a well-known mathematician, but she got a D in Math when she was in high school.
8. The book was lying on the table, which was soaking wet.
10. Rick asked Herb about Herb's pet anaconda.
12. I used to want to be an accountant, but I got a C in accounting, so I changed my mind.
14. I didn't realize that Ben had not read your letter before he called you. His not reading it is what caused all the trouble.
16. In the *New York Times*, the editorial writers say that there is too much vocationalism in higher education.

18. She graduated and joined the navy. Her enlisting surprised me greatly.
20. I took your pants to be cleaned; the cleaners is on my way to school.

### Exercise 23-1: Basic Pronoun Agreement (23a)

2. When a people tell one lie, sooner or later they will need to tell another.
4. You must have confidence in what your spouse is doing when he or she is not with you.
6. Police officers should make sure their uniform is always spotless.
8. A cat often sharpens its claws on the furniture.
10. Newspaper reporters should have their questions written down before they start to interview someone.

### Exercise 23-2: Pronoun Agreement with Compound Antecedents (23c), with Indefinite Pronoun Antecedents (23d) and with Collective Noun Antecedents (23e)

2. Joyce or Fran will lend you her umbrella.
4. The teacher or the students will have to compromise their principles.
6. If you buy avocados or tomatoes, make sure they are ripe.
8. Massachusetts or Michigan cast its electoral votes for Ross Perot.
10. Each of the contestants performed his or her act in three minutes.
12. Someone should donate his or her guitar to the band.
14. Students who works hard in her course will raise their average considerably.
16. The garden really shows its colors in the spring.
18. The association gave its highest award to Paul.
20. The bicycle group knows that the amount of fun it will have depends upon the weather.

### 23-3: Review of Pronoun Agreement

2. Kathy smiled at Audrey, but Audrey looked very solemn when I saw her.

4. Each of the waiters checked his table assignments before leaving for the kitchen.
6. Someone left her umbrella at my apartment.
8. I got my resume typed on a word processor, and after three interviews, I was hired as a data processor for the Social Security Administration. I really appreciated Maxine's help with my job search.
10. Each of the candidates must do his or her own work.
12. Each of the guests brought a plant with him or her.
14. Most of the children could not even write their names.

## Exercise 24-1: Pronoun Case Errors: Subjects vs. Objects (24a), Case After Linking Verbs (24b), and Case in Compound Structures (24c)

2. Whose book is that on the table?
4. Somebody left their book on the table.
6. It became clear to her that the work would be a little harder than she had expected.
8. This project will be shared by us and them.
10. Ernesto and she talked things over calmly.

## Exercise 24-2: Pronoun Case Errors with Appositives (24d) and with *We* and *Us* Before Nouns (24e)

2. My cat vomited on her favorite person in the whole world, me.
4. Maybe we citizens should remember that we elected this president.
6. Even the two best students, Ling and she, couldn't understand the homework last night.
8. If you cooperate during the interview with us reporters for the school paper, you will get good coverage.
10. We sophomores are not used to this kind of treatment.

## Exercise 24-3: Pronoun Case Errors with *Than* and *As* (24f) and *Who* and *Whom* (24g)

2. Herb listens to music more intently than I.
4. As far as I can tell, you are as good at math as she.
6. My mother likes Sylvia better than her.
8. The letter was addressed to "whom it may concern."
10. Doris went to see her grandparents, with whom she enjoys talking.

## Exercise 24-4: Review of Pronoun Case Errors (24a-g)

Peter just received a phone call from a supervisor at a park out west about a position as a volunteer ranger this summer. Peter told the supervisor that it was <u>he</u> who had called earlier to inquire about a position. The supervisor, <u>who</u> sounded quite friendly, said they did need help. Peter said that a friend with <u>whom</u> he had spoken earlier had told him that the work was extremely rigorous. The supervisor said that volunteers who were in good shape would not have any trouble. Peter next asked, "Will <u>we</u> volunteers work six days a week?" The supervisor said yes, but that they would work only half days on Saturdays and Mondays. He had interviewed the volunteers from the previous summer, and, according to <u>them</u>, the job was challenging but rewarding. He urged Peter to send the application back to <u>them</u> as soon as possible.

## Exercise 25-1: Errors with Form of Irregular Verbs (25b)

2. Mr. Alzamora has been sick for a week.
4. Kent has slid safely into third base, but the other team has protested.
6. Bob said that he had given at the office.
8. Jim has broken Debbie's heart.
10. Have you eaten yet?
12. Perhaps I should not have chosen a purple tie with pink roses on it.
14. I think they have hit an all time high.
16. I hate Linda Sadler, and I have felt that way for a long time.
18. These irregular verbs have driven me crazy.
20. I will probably have trouble with these until hell has frozen over.

## Exercise 25-2: Errors with Form of *Lie* and *Lay* (25d) and Omitted *-ed* (25f)

2. You're supposed to come to a complete stop before proceeding through that intersection.
4. Rick used to run much faster than he does now.
6. That darn cat has lain on the couch all afternoon.
8. Every time that happened, I found myself getting depressed.
10. Last night she fixed me a glass of orange juice when we got home.

## Exercise 26-1: Finding and Revising Errors with Verb Tense (26a-d)

2. Before she moved to Stockton, Melia had lived in Japan.
4. Carol Friedman has lived in Manhattan for ten years, but now she is moving to New Jersey.
6. Rose Torres handed me a note and ran back into the bedroom.
8. Chuck had been waiting for two hours when Carla finally showed up.
10. Lance had been on the committee for three years, so they asked him to be the chair.
12. By the time we get to the movie, it will have been showing for a half hour.
14. Paul stood up and yelled for his dog.

## Exercise 26-2: Finding and Revising Errors with Verb Tense (26e and g)

2. I predict that when we get to Jeanine's apartment, she will be reading the homework for tomorrow.
4. More than likely, Joe will be working in his garden as we arrive.
6. The customer who had been rude to the waitress left a large tip.
8. As I was cooking dinner last night, I realized the dog had been barking for at least five minutes.
9. A mistake was made by my math professor, and none of us even noticed.
10. Rosita's boss gave here a $1200 raise.

## Exercise 28-1: Distinguishing Between Adjectives and Adverbs (28a-b)

2. Tawanda felt bad about canceling the party, but she really had no choice.
4. Jennifer opened the door slowly and looked around the empty auditorium.
6. Don't speak too fast when you are delivering your speech.
8. Vergie sings quite well and will probably get a part in the play.
10. My dog smells badly, so he is useless for hunting.

## Exercise 28-2: Comparative and Superlative Forms (28c)

2. Kris was more beautiful in her new dress.
4. Lemons are tangier than limes.

## Exercise 28-3: Avoiding Double Negatives (28d)

2. It's not unusual for it to rain here for several days in a row.
4. I didn't do anything.

## Exercise 29-1: A vs. An (29a)

2. In the refrigerator, you can find an orange or a grapefruit.
4. An orangutan is a lot smaller than a gorilla.
6. Do you know a good Italian restaurant?
8. An elephant is not larger than a whale.

## Exercise 32-1: Recognizing Sentences (32a)

2. The black and white dog with the long tail.
4. Many of the people in the office near me.
6. My boss and her two young children.
8. [My suitcase is too heavy.]
9. Most of the courses at this college.

## Exercise 32-2: Recognizing Fragments (32b)

Being in the army was certainly unpleasant for me. I hated everything I did for those two years. Physical training every morning at six fifteen and inspections almost every Saturday. The boredom was even worse. I spent about five hours a day just waiting. Doing nothing constructive. To make matters worse, my first sergeant hated me. <u>When I first arrived at Fort Bragg.</u> I dropped my rifle on his hoe. <u>Making him my enemy for the next year.</u> He put me on KP every weekend. Now, six years later, I still have nightmares about being in the army.

## Exercise 32-3: Finding and Revising Fragments (32b)

2. AAA is great when you have minor problems such as a flat tire, a dead battery or an overheated engine. I recommend that you become a member.
4. I drove my car without any water in the radiator. As a result, I cracked the engine block. The bill will be more than $500.
6. No fragment
8. Several people have helped Janice get where she is today. For instance, the teacher who encouraged her to play the piano gave her encouragement when she thought of giving up. Also, she was greatly assisted by her brother, who is a fine musician himself.

## Exercise 32-4: Avoiding Comma Splices (32c)

2. I would love a glass of ice water. My mouth is dry.
4. My boss just quit. He is moving to Houston.
6. Until I hear from Danali, I am not writing her another letter.
8. Ms. Macrae's job is exciting. She is a reporter for Channel 11.
10. Eugene's cake was terrible. He forgot the eggs.

## Exercise 32-5: Avoiding Run-Ons (32c)

2. These marbles are valuable. They are more than one hundred years old.
4. My father grew up in a small town in Georgia. Hortense still does not have any traffic lights.
6. Alexis is moving to New York. She found a great job.
8. Ms. Hesler walked into the room and handed back the papers.
10. Dave Berry did well in his chemistry course. He likes doing experiments.

## Exercise 32-6: Review of Avoiding Fragments, Run-ons, and Comma Splices

Work is a hard word to define. It has too many different meanings. It seems to mean anything that requires an expenditure of energy, like carrying furniture or unloading ships. However, some kinds of work don't involve expending energy. I'm thinking of computer programming or accounting, unless you count mental energy. On the other hand, some activities that expend a lot of energy are not really work. Playing tennis takes a lot of energy, especially the way I play. However, it's not considered work. Maybe work is anything you get paid for doing. That would cover computer programming and accounting, and it would not include tennis. However, it also would not include chopping wood or shoveling snow, which both seem like a lot of work to me. It also would include winning the lottery or inheriting a million dollars. Neither of these is really work.

## Exercise 33-1: Using Commas and Coordinating Conjunctions to Join Independent Clauses (33a)

2. I can write my paper on Friday, or I can stay home on Sunday and do it.
4. Theresa will fix dinner for all of us, or we can go out to Milano's.
6. We will put our furniture in storage and sell the house.
8. An airplane flew low over the stadium and dropped leaflets on the crowd.
10. I had not ordered a pizza, but the manager at Domino's insisted that I had.

## Exercise 33-2: Using Semicolons to Join Independent Clauses (33b)

2. I loved the movie last night; it was about my hometown.
4. Please hand me a pot holder; they are in the top, left-hand drawer.
6. My calculus class was canceled this morning; the teacher is sick.
8. Arnie had never seen a sheep before; he grew up in the city.
10. This has been a terrible day; I lost my purse on the bus.

## Exercise 33-3: Punctuating Sentences with Conjunctive Adverbs (33c)

2. I had already seen the movie; however, I didn't mind seeing it again.
4. Rita forgot her umbrella; as a result, she got completely soaked.
6. The food is much better at the Stone Inn; also, there is plenty of parking.
8. The new apartment had two bathrooms; as a result, we could all sleep fifteen minutes later in the mornings.
10. Gerry put away the groceries; meanwhile, Nancy made a salad.
12. We ordered a spinach salad; instead, the waiter brought us spinach pie.
14. The parking lot was full; consequently, we parked across the street.

## Exercise 33-4: Punctuating Compound Complex Sentences (33d)

2. But then a warm spell arrived, which perhaps was all the trees and flowers were waiting for, and it seemed like there was no stopping Mother Nature after that.
4. Many people were relieved to see the plants doing so well, since ice storms during the winter had been so damaging.

## Exercise 33-5: Review of Using Commas and Semicolons to Punctuate Independent Clauses

2. "I'll be on the east coast for a few days next month; consequently, I might drop in and see you," my friend Henry wrote to me.
4. Julie had studied hard and knew the material; however, she was not good at taking tests under pressure.
6. Nothing happened when I mixed the chemicals together; therefore, my experiment was a failure.
8. When I looked out the window an hour later, the kids were still playing their games, and the parents remained nearby.
10. We went to a matinee, so we could save on the admission price.

## Exercise 34-1: Using Commas with Introductory Elements (34a)

2. To join the Jaycees, he had to pay a lot of money.
4. While she was looking carefully in the ditch, she spotted the wounded quail.
6. Checking the dictionary is the only way to be sure about spelling.
8. To get a camping spot on the fourth of July is almost impossible in Yosemite.
10. To be accepted to the Naval Academy was quite an honor.
12. Looking down, I didn't see Joanie. She was just getting home from her trip.
14. To my way of thinking, we should invite the entire class to the party.

## Exercise 34-2: Using Commas with Items in a Series (34b)

2. Debbie, Linda, and Theresa are going to California for the summer.
4. Leslie put mothballs in her suitcases, in her closet, and in her footlocker.
6. Airlines, trains, and buses were delayed by this weekend's snowstorm.
8. I found sand in my pockets, in my purse, and in my ears when I got back from the beach.
10. The high jump, the discus throw, and the pole vault are my favorite events in the Olympics.

## Exercise 34-3: Using Commas with Restrictive and Non-Restrictive Clauses, Phrases, and Appositives (34c)

2. This sentence is correct.
4. Fireworks exploding overhead is an entrancing sight.
6. This sentence is correct.
8. The outfielder, running hard to her right, made an outstanding backhanded catch.
10. That book, *Great Expectations*, has been a favorite for more than 100 years.

## Exercise 34-4: Using Commas to Set Off Parenthetical Expressions, Nouns of Direct Address, Yes and No, Interjections, and Tag Questions (34d)

2. Mr. Speaker, will you let me have the floor?
4. That's a dangling modifier, isn't it?

6. Well don't look at me, I didn't leave the light on all night.
8. She's a good dog, in my opinion, as long as you give her enough exercise.
10. Yes, I'll help you mow the grass, even though I'm busy right now.

## Exercise 34-5: Using Commas with Coordinate and Cumulative Adjectives (34e) and Absolute Phrases (34f)
2. Monica loves her new lightweight cordless phone.
4. Barbar's stubborn, old horse would not come down to the barn.
6. It having rained earlier, the air was humid.
8. The test was more difficult than she expected, so Sherry, wanting to get a good grade in the class, decided she would study more.
10. The trip, extensively researched and planned, turned out well.

## Exercise 34-6: Using Commas with Contrasted Elements (34g) and with Quotations (34h)
2. Unlike the maples, the sycamores held up fairly well in the storm.
4. The car I have now, unlike my previous one, drives well.
6. "I think the council does not listen to the people," she told the reporter.
8. "Because they don't care what the people think," she said. "They're going to do what they want no matter what.
10. "The vote two weeks ago," she said, "when everybody at the public hearing spoke against that road project, but they passed it anyway, is an example."

## Exercise 34-7: Using Commas with Dates and Places (34i)
2. The Allied Company has asked for a delivery date in November 1993.
4. Lenny, Marc, and Bill were all hired on 30 August 1989.
6. Clifford Still began work on this painting in May 1981, and completed it in August of that year.
8. Do you know what happened on December 7, 1941?

10. As of 1 January 1995, I will never make another error.

## Exercise 34-8: Review of Comma Rules (32c, 33a, and 34)
2. Gino wrote a paper on computerized reservation systems for hotels; he is studying to be a computer programmer.
4. I can't go with you to the movies, for I am completely out of cash.
6. Lara, Gary, and Jim are working together on their papers this weekend.
8. My father, who works for a bakery, is bringing two loaves of olive bread, a pie, and a cake to the party tonight.
10. Maurice stood up suddenly and hit his head on the bookshelf.
12. Denine brought a wet, exhausted dog into the house last night.
14. You can write to the museum at 11308 South Rim Road, Omaha, Nebraska 58902.
16. The man who gave me a ride to work this morning was a friend of my music teacher.
18. Corey fixed Eva a cup of coffee and a bagel for breakfast.
20. Maeshon is quite angry with Andy; he forgot her birthday last week.

## Exercise 35-1: Forming Possessive Nouns (35a)
2. Several teachers were eating lunch in the student union.
4. The President's speech to Congress was misleading.
6. Several police officers' cars were vandalized.
10. Can you tell me where the women's room is located?
12. The two deer's antlers became locked during their battle.
14. Nelson was awakened by sixty sheep's bleating.

## Exercise 35-2: Contractions (35c)
2. My essay isn't finished, but I'm not worried about it.
4. My sister won't let me open doors for her.

130

6. I wonder what they're going to do when their daughter doesn't come home from college for the summer.
8. I don't like asparagus.
10. What's for dinner tonight?

## Exercise 35-3: Confusion of Contractions and Possessives (35e)
2. I got my application in the mail, but Marlene hasn't gotten hers.
4. I hear you're going to San Francisco this weekend.
6. Tony's dog hurt its leg, but it's better now.
8. It's a shame that the election is being held so early.
10. I don't know anyone who's going to the dance.

## Exercise 35-4: Review of Apostrophes (35)
Just once in my life, I would like to take an extreme position. However, on every issue I can think of, I end up in the middle of the road. I have come to the conclusion that I am compulsively moderate.

At my job I disapprove of people who can only say "yes" to the boss. I think people should have the courage to express their opinions even when those opinions are different from the boss's. On the other hand, there are two men at work who seem to disagree with everything our boss says. They waste everyone's time by objecting to every decision. Their negative attitudes are disruptive. So once again, I approve of a little rebelliousness, but not too much.

Of course, moderation is all right in its place. My problem is that I am always moderate. I can never take an extreme position. You might say that I'm extremely moderate, but, at least, that means I've found something that I'm extreme about.

## Exercise 36-1: Quotations (36)
2. "I'll be here when you get back," he said. "I won't be gone long," she replied. "Well, I might miss you anyway."
4. "While My Guitar Genlty Weeps" is one of Susan's Cat's favorite Beatles songs.

6. The "shower" we just had was closer to a monsoon.
8. One student said, "Sometimes I can't remember if periods go inside of quotation marks or out."
10. "What are some differences between Hemingway's style and Fitzgerald's?" was the test question.

## Exercise 37-1: Colons, Ellipses, Parentheses, Brackets, Dashes and Slashes (37)
2. One the desk were some envelopes, a pencil and a coffee cup.
4. "Each year, after the midwinter blizzards, there comes a night of thaw when the tinkle of dripping water is heard . . ." (Leopold, 3).
6. Mark's mother called him and said that "[she] would arrive next Monday."
8. If you cannot/will not attend the meeting, please let me know.

## Exercise 38-1: Capitalization (38)
I have an uncle who seems to have figured out the secret to being happy. About twenty years ago, he was a doctor making lots of money and working seventy hours a week. One day, he announced he was quitting his practice and living for himself from then on. When he had been in college, he had worked his way through school by renovating houses, mostly for his friends. Now that he has quit medicine, he had gone back to what he always enjoyed most—renovation. He works only about four days a week and takes a vacation for two months every winter. Last year he flew to Florida and rented a sailboat. He and his Irish setter just sailed east into the ocean for a month and then sailed back for a month. Then he was ready to go back to his work with a fresh outlook. The combination of doing a job he loves and not working very hard seems to guarantee that he is always happy.

## Exercise 44-1: Editing for Spelling Errors (44b)
2. It never occurred to me that I would receive a grant.
4. I was loving the play until the third act, which was too depressing.

6. Sook Moon <u>worried</u> so much that it was noticeable to everyone.
8. Tawanda couldn't <u>conceive</u> of someone being so mean.
10. Maria's new car does not get better <u>mileage</u> than her old one.

**Exercise 44-2: Editing for Spelling Errors (44c)**
2. Jackie had to get four <u>inoculations</u> for her trip.
4. Consuela is not ready for <u>marriage</u>, but her boyfriend is.
6. Can you <u>appreciate</u> the awkwardness of my position?
8. We hope to <u>develop</u> a faster way to calculate the company's profits.
10. Jeremy did not intend to start a <u>quarrel</u>.

**Exercise 44-3: Finding words in a Dictionary When You Don't Know How to Spell Them (44d)**
2. chelate
4. incubus

**Exercises 44-4: Editing for Spelling Errors (44f)**
2. Hank is on good terms with all three of his former <u>wives</u>.
4. A connection between coffee and cancer was not established in either of our <u>studies</u>.
6. We found our kitten hiding under some <u>bushes</u>.
8. Several <u>deer</u> have been hit by cars on this road.
10. A bouquet of <u>lilies</u> was sitting on the mantle.

**Exercise 44-5: Review of Spelling (44a-f)**
2. Were you <u>listening</u> when Ray Cisneros announced he was applying for the job?
4. I would never have time to read a <u>daily</u> paper.
6. Oliver usually <u>ridicules</u> people who make mistakes.
8. Tien tried to <u>persuade</u> Martha to go to the movies with her.

10. The <u>beginning</u> of this exercise created a <u>dilemma</u> for me.